Advanced Praise Page

"A lovely case study for anyone who works with people and organizations, and a treat for those who admire the Rolling Stones for their music and career achievements."—Professor Robert Eccles, Visiting Professor of Management Practice, Said Business School, University of Oxford

"Start Me Up and Keep Me Growing by Bertold Bär-Bouyssiere is not just a most important, smart and enjoyable book, but one that would give you profound understanding of the intricacies of the modern human condition and lessons for the times to come. Competitiveness is at the heart of human nature at any organizational level: states, political parties, businesses or musical associations. We admire how the key individuals of the Stones were able to maintain an equilibrium of power for such a long time, and we also admire the wisdom of the others who helped in making this adventure last."—Professor Dr. Alexander Mirtchev, LLM, PhD, Vice-Chair of the Atlantic Council of US, President Krull Corporation

"Bertold has written a witty, enjoyable and relatable book for anyone running a growth business. Whether still in the garage or already gone viral, this book will be a page-turner for start-up entrepreneurs and leaders of mature businesses alike. Whether it's about articulating your vision, getting initial traction, hyper-scaling or staying the course, Bertold's decades of experience as a legal counsellor, technician, rainmaker and then elected board member of a global professional services firm, are lovingly translated through the eyes of a lifelong Rolling Stones fan. 'Start Me Up and Keep Me Growing' is not just for law firm partners, but for anyone building a growth business, especially startup founders."—Louis Lehot, Partner, Foley & Lardner

"Great to read about the Stones from a business angle. Discipline, team-work, creative and financial ingenuity, exactly what all professional services firms are all about!"—Todd Seelman, Managing Partner Denver, Lewis Brisbois

START ME UP AND KEEP ME GROWING

START ME UP AND KEEP ME GROWING

MANAGEMENT LEARNINGS FROM
THE ROLLING STONES

BY BERTOLD
BÄR-BOUYSSIERE

ANTHEM PRESS

FIRST HILL BOOKS

An imprint of Wimbledon Publishing Company Limited (WPC)

This edition first published in UK and USA 2022
by FIRST HILL BOOKS
75–76 Blackfriars Road, London SE1 8HA, UK
or PO Box 9779, London SW19 7ZG, UK

and
244 Madison Ave #116, New York, NY 10016, USA

British Library Cataloguing-in-Publication Data
A catalogue record for this book is available from the British Library.

Library of Congress Control Number: 2022932214

ISBN-13: 978-1-83998-495-2 (Pbk)
ISBN-10: 1-83998-495-3 (Pbk)

This title is also available as an e-book.

"All this time some central force beyond music or money must have held us together."
Bill Wyman, Stone Alone

This book is dedicated to my mother, my wife Sabine, and my sons David and Samuel and to the memory of my father and parents-in-law.

CONTENTS

WHAT TO EXPECT FROM THIS BOOK
AND HOW TO USE IT (INTRO)

At least half of the people living on this planet have heard of the world's greatest rock 'n' roll band, a professional services firm that has been supplying musical services and related entertainment services internationally for 60 years, in response to growing demand that does not seem to dry up.

What began as a musical project to bring the Afro-American blues to a white UK audience developed into one of the greatest musical legacies of the century, comprised of songs in a wide variety of styles, and continues to draw crowds in the millions, who pay hefty ticket prices to watch the band perform their songs on stage. On the side, the project created sizable personal fortunes that rank in the top of their industry.

Since my early teenage years in the 1970s I have been a fan of the Stones, and I never get tired of listening to their music. Their repertoire has songs for every situation of life, from joyful ecstasy to the deepest sorrow. Their music has carried me through times of joy, success, loss, and mourning.

Sometimes I wonder whether King David, whose 150 psalms dealt with life from all angles, would have loved the music of the Stones if he could have heard it, and I also occasionally think that the immediately recognizable musical DNA that constitutes the basis of every Stones song could be quite a good soundtrack for the lyrics of David's psalms.

Music is one of my passions—I played the cello in amateur orchestras up to age 30—but I also work as a commercially minded lawyer, that is, a service provider who aims at giving his clients the service of quality that they deserve. Based on my own professional experience the biggest challenge in any professional association is the aspect of interpersonal dynamics. The human condition is to be competitive, and competitiveness involves comparison with others. Paradoxically, the more an enterprise is successful, the more difficult it is to manage the human aspect. In an emergency people seek each other's support;

solidarity is at its peak. As soon as the storm has calmed down the same people resume competing. Most partnerships break up after some time because people don't get along with each other anymore. Or members leave firms for the same reason.

Partnership-based professional services firms have many things in common with rock bands, in particular, the interdependence of their members. In both types of firms, people are the key assets. Changing the drummer in a band is more impactful than replacing one real estate partner in a large law firm, but such change still has an impact. Any organization will need to find the right balance between the gain from innovating and transforming, including through peoples' management, and the cost of destroying a fabric of people that has a woven track record of professional interaction. While there is no management principle that fits all sizes, it is reassuring when decisions are taken for the right reasons.

Having evolved for more than 25 years in large law firms in both client-facing and internal supervisory roles, I occasionally found it difficult to evaluate a business decision submitted for approval. One day I came to ask myself whether inspiration can be found in the success story of the Stones. In writing this short business and management history of the Stones, my objective was to identify the factors that determined the evolution of the Stones as a professional services organization. The focus is on themes relevant for organizational wisdom, such as the following: How do you get a business started? How does leadership emerge, and at what cost is it followed by others? How does one cope with a business venture that outgrows all expectations? How are important decisions taken, such as changing the manager or adapting the business to an evolving environment? How to preserve the business against external and internal threats? How are the members incentivized, rewarded, or sanctioned in the event of failure, and how much room is there for democratic decision making as opposed to top-down leadership? The most difficult one: How do you keep your people together?

Members of professional services firms can always pull out with their book of business and plug it in a different place to carry on. For members of the world's greatest rock 'n' roll band that step is not easily taken—and yet it happened. One of the founding band members left after 30 years to pursue other opportunities, and another replacement-hire quit after 5 years, suffering from what today is called a burnout. Several others stayed together for 45 to 60 years, but it was far from easy both for the more dominating characters and for those in supporting roles. The essence of the question was, "How much shit-taking is this whole thing worth to me?" The more vocational and profitable a venture, the bigger the incentive to endure. It took the individual Stones members many years to fully grasp the level of their interdependence, from which there was no escape short of nuclear destruction. We ordinary mortals working in our businesses can learn from them.

How can you read and make use of this book? Maybe you are just a Stones fan who wants to read a business history of the Stones. You should enjoy your read. Maybe you are a member of one of the many professional services firms. In that case, much of what you will read will resonate and echo your own experience. Maybe you are a talent developer in the human resources department of a large corporate organization. You may find some food for thought in here.

The same may apply to teachers in business schools. The idea of this book emerged when my former firm invited me to a week of training in the prestigious Harvard Business School (HBS) in 2012. It was a fantastic experience. I learned and enjoyed the case study approach. The director in charge of the program was Professor Bob G. Eccles, one of the key drivers behind integrated reporting. He was open to do a case study about the Stones, but it failed for two reasons: By the time I had the "basic track" covering the entire career of the Stones, Professor Eccles had left the school. The second reason was that there was no way I could squeeze the entire Stones' history into the HBS format of 10 pages. In other words, the main body of this book is an oversized case study. It is written in factual, if not elliptic, style.

This book may also serve as inspiration to business founders in the launch phase of their start-up. It is very short and can be read in a few hours on a train or plane.

I do hope that all readers will sense the pneuma between the lines and seize the meaning of the story told. It is an amazing story by all possible standards, and I am grateful that I had the time to tell it.

My main sources are the books of Philip Norman and Christopher Sandford. I used them to lay down the "basic track," which I subsequently overdubbed. They were helpful in getting the chronology right and contained many juicy quotes that I picked up here, properly referenced. One of the most insightful books about the Stones is Victor Bockris's biography of Keith. Other important sources were the memoirs of Andrew Oldham and Prince Rupert. Marianne Faithfull's memoirs were also helpful. Over the last 20 years, I have been a daily reader of Keno's Gasland, one of the best fan sites that were active until a few years ago. I owe Keno and the contributors to his site many valuable insights. To Keno goes a particular thank you. Finally, in almost 50 years as a Stones fan I have picked up much stuff here and there which I happen to remember, except that I forgot where I read it. As they say, "It's Only Rock 'n' Roll (But I Like It)."

Enough said. Enjoy your read.

Brussels, April 20, 2022

A. ROCK BAND INTERPERSONAL WORKPLACE DYNAMICS

In the main body of this text, readers will find a short business history of the Rolling Stones. It is a condensed selection of episodes covering a career spanning 60 years. The interrogation beneath the choice of episodes is to understand how a rock band can stay together for such a long period and achieve such a planetary and unprecedented success. My own professional experience showed me how difficult it is for a firm to be successful in the long term without producing interpersonal fallouts, collateral casualties so to say. Hence my quest to find out whether firms in general, and professional services firms in particular, can learn from the Rolling Stones' experience, and if so, what. The conclusion is that indeed there is much to learn, if only because men and women working in different industries are not fundamentally different. There are anthropological commonalities between workers cross-sector, and the interpersonal psychodynamics are very much the same. This is true Nnot only in private businesses but also in public administrations.

Before delving into the incredible history of the Rolling Stones, an attempt will be made to identify different working patterns in the rock act industry and to develop a high-level typology of rock acts. Just as there are different types of professional services firms in any given sector, there are different types of organizational patterns among those who create and perform the music that rejoices millions of people in the Western world and beyond. In the legal services industry for example, the range of organizational patterns is wide, from the solo practitioner via the boutique firm to the global law firm. Even among the larger structures there are different organizational patterns: business law firms, magic circle firms, elite firms, and so on, and each type of firm tends to favor a particular way of organizational structure and remuneration policy, from lockstep to merit-based to eat-what-you-kill. Even between firms of similar type, fundamental differences can be found in terms of management style (corporate top-down or partnership-based democracy), the way in which work is channeled by management and the way in which remuneration of members is determined. Each type of firm, if not every firm, creates its own pattern of interpersonal dynamics, and the psychological disposition of the members' personalities is a determining factor in the way in which a firm evolves. As in any organization, the psychological disposition of the leaders will have the biggest impact on firm development, but the psychodynamics of the partner base cannot be ignored either.

Looking at the rock acts we have known for many years similarities are obvious. In the music industry it is possible to distinguish different career paths and organizational patterns.

One of them is the solo artist. A solo artist with a career almost as long and successful as the Stones is David Bowie. David was one of the most talented pop artists, and his long career has produced a remarkable legacy of memorable songs. Hence, not only his organizational choice but also his artistic project differs from that of the Rolling Stones in several respects. Those familiar with David's work appreciate the almost forgotten recordings of his earliest period, with songs such as "Maid of Bond Street," "Join the Gang," and "She's Got Medals." These songs are as diverse as they are beautiful, charming with a touch of vaudeville. Unfortunately for David, the album was a commercial flop. This led to an impressive turnaround in David's marketing approach and to the creation of an artificial personae "Ziggy Stardust," who brought David's music the attention that it deserved. The advantage of the artificial personae is that it can be easily changed to adapt to changed market conditions. Indeed, in the mid-1970s, when glam rock was dying and punk was on the rise, David invented the "Thin White Duke." He looked great in this role, with his short blond hair, and his voice had matured and gained gravitas—best evidenced on the excellent double-live album *Stage* (1978). His theater-like shows from the 1980s confirmed though that in David's project music was a vehicle for something else, that is, the staging of his personality. This very personal project culminated in David's unprecedented staging of his death through the *Black Star* album and its related videos. While before David, Freddy Mercury and several others had found a way of saying goodbye to their fan community (e.g., Queen's moving album *The Show Must Go On*), their goodbye was mostly expressed in traditional musical forms. David's path was different. For everyone who had not yet understood it from the many hints and signs throughout his career, the final videos made it clear that David's project was a gnostic spiritual pilgrimage that involved salvation through a process of self-realization as a "star." Quite a difference from Charlie's discreet checking out. In that process, music had a serving role, albeit an important one. This contrasts with the Stones' project, where music is a goal in itself. If the Rolling Stones project also has a spiritual dimension, it was not there at the outset and only evolved over time. Furthermore, should the Stones attribute a redemptive power to music at all, music is all that is preached (cf. "Hot Stuff" and "It's Only Rock 'n' Roll").

As a genuine solo artist, David collaborated with others, some of whom contributed much to his artistic success (e.g., Tony Visconti). Nevertheless, David could change his collaborators whenever he deemed fit, and he did change them quite frequently. This probably saved him the painful interpersonal experiences that characterized the career of the Stones who had to learn to accept each other and to find a sustainable interpersonal balance. On the other hand, it deprived David of the benefit of evolving with a true band, and it had an impact on the work product. Working with hired musicians favors conventional recording processes, and the result is conventionally produced music. His earlier albums contain wonderful musical figures and songs of great architecture with impressive dramaturgy. However, in later years, there seems to be an occasional temptation at work of patching together, albeit intelligently, pre-existing modules of musical expression. Further, even when song and voice are great, it does not matter which musicians play on it. There are probably few people who stretch their ears to figure out the bass line of a song or the drums, as there is no reason to zoom in on a studio musician who played just on this one album. This is not Bill and Charlie speaking their unique language. Whether on album or on stage, it is all about David.

Another challenge for all long-term solo artists is that they must do everything themselves. Solo artists are alone when creating the music and must themselves conduct the organization of its recording. Sound engineers and studio musicians will execute instructions given. The decision-maker is alone and has no equal partner serving as soundboard. Further, long-term creativity is a delicate flower, and solo artists do not benefit from collective processes of co-creation and mutual editing that comes with band acts. In David's later years, the best albums are those where he reconnected with Tony Visconti, his partner from earlier collaborations.

There are other solo acts whose patterns differ slightly. Elton John, another longtime rock act with planetary success, collaborates with lyricist Bernie Taupin. Their collaboration has lasted for decades and contributed greatly to Elton's success. Elton's project, like the Stones, is all about the music, not his personality. The same goes for many other piano-based solo artists such as Billy Joel or Randy Newman, who place a greater emphasis on socially relevant lyrics.

At the next organizational level are bands. At closer look there are rock bands with differing organizational patterns. First there are bands by design. These are bands designed by a producer in the context of a commercial project where the producer himself selects future band members to fit into his commercial project. According to Barney Hoskin's *Hotel California*, the Eagles fall into this category. Rock mogul David Geffen casted them to continue the lucrative stream of folk-rock music originating in the LA Canyons scene. The Eagles worked out well and had a fantastic career.

Another pattern is the single-person band. It looks like a band, but there is one dominating individual who drives it all. Paul McCartney's Wings were such a band. Another example is Jethro Tull. Flutist Ian Anderson was its dominant personality. The irony is that most teenagers in the 1970s did not care for Ian's flute but preferred the guitar riffs of long-term band member Martin Barre (e.g., "Locomotive Breath" and "Aqualung"). Many remember his riffs, few remember his name. Other than him, the lineup was constantly changed. A variant of this category is the support band which mostly works in support of one prominent artist, such as Bruce Springsteen's E Street Band.

Bands in this category are less known for interpersonal tensions because the members submit to the dominating personality from the outset. Also, these bands can be long-lived, because the dominant member can substitute other band members at will.

The third category is that of the true band with a genuinely collective artistic project and a high degree of collective songwriting. There were many great true bands emerging in the 1960s and 1970s, including the Who, the Small Faces, Deep Purple to Roxy Music, Yes, Supertramp, and many more in more recent years, such as Guns N' Roses to name just one. The Beatles and the Stones also belong to this category.

There seems to be an unwritten rule for all these bands that the bigger the interpersonal tensions, the better the musical output. Not surprisingly, the greatest novels come from Russia and not from Switzerland. Another unwritten rule is that most of these bands are short-lived, because the members do not have the endurance required to support the editorial constraint exercised by the others. The Beatles are the best example for this tendency. Clearly the most talented of all bands, almost touching the Mozart-like inexplicable, they produced the single most important sing-along song catalogue of the twentieth century. Songs that today's kids whistle without knowing who the Beatles even were. Anyone who attends an evening show of the Parrots, a Japanese Beatles Tribute band achieving 99 percent of resemblance with the original, in Tokyo's

Abbey Road club in Roppongi[1] can experience the magic of the Beatles' compositions. When they start "While My Guitar ... ," the audience sheds a tear. Not even a Rolling Stones concert has this psychological impact.

The Beatles like the Stones were built around two central contributors, with a third in the wings. Admittedly, George Harrison was more successful in getting his songs on his band's albums than Bill, but despite the unmatched quality of his songs he had to fight for them. Further, in the case of the Beatles, it is easier to identify the main author of a song, because the author would typically sing the lead vocals. Many songs are clearly identifiable as Lennon or McCartney songs. Each of them had the ability to take a song from inception to album, and their interdependence may have been lower or they may have believed it to be lower. However, there are also stories of John and Paul building up songs together. When Paul wrote "It's getting better all the time," John added "It can't get no worse" ("Getting Better"). Paul being a more robust personality and John suffering from insecurities, tensions quickly built up. When each of them married a woman with a strong motherly personality, the band cohesion suffered. Unlike Paul's Linda John's Yoko was—unjustly— diabolized by the others, maybe because she was foreign. While her art is occasionally eccentric for Western ears (and maybe for Japanese ears too), her courage to move from a traditional bourgeois family to America in the 1960s to pursue an artistic career is remarkable. And some of her more conventionally performed songs are surprisingly good and maybe even better than some of John's solo efforts. For the past five decades, the mantra has been that Paul decided one day that he did not need the Beatles anymore, and he quit.[2] The rest is history. George produced some highlights but quickly exhausted his talent. John Lennon's albums up to *Walls and Bridges* contain a few gems but mostly very average material. It is a double tragedy that John was brutally murdered just after finishing his musically best and most joyfully optimistic album ever, *Double Fantasy*, starting with the Roy Orbison–like "Starting Over"; it contained as many quality songs by John as by Yoko. Paul's solo efforts are very solid pop up to today. However, there are not many songs that reach the emotional greatness of "Eleanor Rigby." Further, he tends to play many instruments himself, which is not always sparkling. Paul or John may have thought that they did not need the Beatles but in fact they did. Their output was best when John and Paul exercised a mutual editorial constraint

---

1 I owe this experience to my former GW Law classmate and friend Masaki Hata.

2 The new Peter Jackson documentary may revise this mantra.

on each other. Curiously, Ringo Starr, the world's most underrated drummer, has done unexpectedly well in his solo career, producing many very solid and enjoyable records. It is the sad fate of those assuming the role of the joker that nobody listens to them, although they may be the wisest.

The Rolling Stones are well ranked in both the quality and the longevity contests. Both are linked. Bill once complained that most of the great Stones hits are from the early period. What he meant was that his songs would bring the Stones back in the charts. Some of Bill's songs did indeed climb high in the charts, but they did not conform to the Stones' musical direction, which was determined in between Mick and Keith. Not only Bill but critics also complained that the Stones never innovated radically since their great U-turn from psychedelic back to basic rock in 1968. These critics are both right and wrong. The Stones never went fully experimental, prog rock, or symphonic. At the same time, while sticking to their blues roots, the Stones did occasionally try new sounds and recording techniques to stay connected with the Zeitgeist, such as on *Emotional Rescue* (the title song), *Undercover* ("Too Much Blood"), and *Bridges to Babylon* ("Might As Well Get Juiced"). Overall, however, there is a long-term consistency which makes the music immediately recognizable, including the playing style of the instrumentalists. A careful listener immediately spots Keith, Ron, or Charlie and even Bill when they support other artists' records. No one else has described this better than French journalist Alain Wais when he saluted the release of *Dirty Work* in France's newspaper *Le Monde* on March 25, 1986: nobody expects anything else from the Rolling Stones but a Rolling Stones record—hoping that it is better than the previous one and less bad than the next one.[3] Ironically, as shall be seen later in this book, he wrote in the same article (in simplified translation), "The Stones must have enjoyed the recording; despite the many invitees, they haven't sounded as joined up in a long time." He could not have been more wrong. Paradoxically, it was exactly when the feud between Mick and Keith peaked at its worst, with the band on the verge of breaking up, that the Stones delivered their most energetic and raw album in a decade. Thus, maximum stress and quality of output frequently go hand in hand.

Most interestingly, there was another article on the front page of *Le Monde* on the same day, by Michel Braudeau, celebrating in no less enthusiastic terms the same album and adding nostalgically that even if the Stones were never to

---

3 https://www.lemonde.fr/archives/article/1986/03/25/vingt-cinquieme-anniversaire -des-rolling-stones-dirty-work-avec-plaisir_3116007_1819218.html.

play again (it is frightening how close he was to the truth), their simple existence guaranteed a dream of eternal youth. To have two articles with contradictory spins on the front page of *Le Monde* on the same day in 1986 about an album release and a 25th band anniversary is quite an achievement.[4] This was more than 35 years ago, and the Stones are still touring albeit, sadly, without the late Charlie. They must have got something right. But what and how is the object of this book.

To what extent is all this relevant to professional services firms and other types of businesses? They are also ventures with a beginning, a life curve, and an end. They frequently start as small partnerships but can become very big. Being peoples' organizations, the interpersonal dynamics play a significant role. The key difference is that they are built to last beyond the lifetime of the founders, which is assured by proper succession planning. For their No Filter Tour the Stones could have Steve Jordan take Charlie's seat, but this replacement pattern has its limits. Other than that, there are many similarities. Members aspire to responsibilities, respect, recognition, and remuneration. There are struggles for power and influence. Human nature has been largely the same since we descended from the trees. Competitiveness and jealousy are central features of it. To invoke a biblical story, as soon as God had created humans, Adam and Eve made their biggest mistake and lost paradise. Their offspring, the first-ever pair of brothers, ended in Abel's murder by Cain. But why did Cain, a farmer, murder his brother Abel, a shepherd? Cain the farmer became jealous when he thought that God favored Abel's offering over his. Similarly, professional jealousy made Salieri, who had vowed his chastity to God in exchange for talent, poison the much more talented but so frivolous Mozart, as shown in Miloš Forman's *Amadeus*. Further, Cain may have been driven by an erroneous perception, a mere supposition. Given the fallibility of interpersonal communications, how often do we read a bad intention into a well-intended message. When someone greets us with the words "You look great today!" we ask back "Did I not look great yesterday?"; or the question "How are you doing today?" provokes the answer "Why? Do I look tired?"

The same type of jealousy is at work in firms when members are promoted to leadership positions to which colleagues aspired as well. Or when there is a perception that the annual bonus is not allocated based on merit but on

---

4 https://www.lemonde.fr/archives/article/1986/03/25/le-travail-des-anges_2923808_1819218.html.

political grounds. Or where newly appointed leaders exit those they have been competing with. Thus, in terms of interpersonal dynamics, the bridge from Abel and Cain via Salieri and Mozart and Jagger and Richards to all of us is not that long.

Enough said. Curtain up!

B. IT'S NOT ONLY ROCK 'N' ROLL

Part One—Turning Vision into Talent (1962–1968)

1. Genesis

On July 12, 1962, Brian Jones, Mick Jagger, Keith Richards, Ian Stewart, and two other musicians performed three songs originally by Jimmy Reed, Muddy Waters, and Chuck Berry in London's Marquee Club, located in Soho's Wardour Street. They called themselves Rolling Stones, after Muddy Waters's "*Rollin' Stone*" (according to Keith) or a line in Muddy Waters's "Mannish Boy" (Mick's version). It was Brian who had chosen the name. This was the beginning of a great adventure that at the time of writing will have lasted no less than 60 years. It took many different ingredients to achieve this planetary success, ranging from creativity, passion, camaraderie, and friendship to ambition, ruthlessness, power lust, and money hunger. Other ingredients are/were courage, determination, discipline, fairness, solidarity, discipline, competitiveness, and innovativeness. These will become apparent as we move through the main narrative.

Typically, even a radical innovation does not emerge out of nothingness but has its roots in the Zeitgeist. When the Stones started their own musical venture, they could build on an infrastructure for musical ventures. The infrastructure in the case at hand was the well-developed club scene that, even where it catered to different musical tastes, was hungry for new acts to keep them running. And people wanted music and the different sorts of pleasure and excitement that derive from it. London's Marquee Club belonged to the National Jazz League, whose moving spirit at that time was Chris Barber, one of Britain's most influential musicians for more than a decade in those years still close to the experience of World War II. Barber led Britain's commercially most successful Dixieland band but remained at the same time a passionate searcher for overlooked gems and traditions.

He was a musical archaeologist like what Keith Richards would later evolve into. Barber's 1954-released LP *New Orleans Joys* had included two blues songs played in skiffle style with Lonnie Donegan on banjo, setting off a national passion for holding and playing a matchwood guitar, while being accompanied by washboards and basses improvised from tea chests and wire.[1] It was not exactly the sort of music the Stones would soon begin to promote. However, soon after, Tommy Steele, a British merchant seaman, would dock at Norfolk, the United States, hear Buddy Holly, and become Britain's first rock 'n' roller.

Back then the world was much less globalized than it is today, but culture, like trade, knew no boundaries. Moreover, as at any time in human history, the importation of foreign cultural elements, whether in the form of a style or a foreign-born individual, enriched domestic cultural life. One of those foreign and exotic elements was Alexis Korner, a musician of Austrian, Greek, Russian, and Turkish descent. He was born in Paris and spent his early childhood years in Switzerland and Morocco before moving to London's St Paul School. When walking from his Ealing home to Shepherd's Bush Market, he came across a record by blues pianist Jimmy Yancey and only wanted to become a boogie-woogie pianist from then on. During his military service in West Germany, he became an AFN radio announcer, broadcasting jazz, swing, and blues for NATO bases all over Europe.[2] Alexis replaced Lonnie Donegan during the latter's military service in the Chris Barber band, playing banjo skiffle style. He declined to join a commercially promising skiffle band signed up by EMI executive George Martin and created the Alexis Korner's Blues Incorporated, the first band in Britain to play nothing but blues—a music that only a few passionate aficionados were listening to. The sad-faced part-time drummer's name was Charlie Watts, a student of commercial art in Harrow. Toward the end of 1961, a broadly built boy in a smart Italian suit walked up to Korner, talking authoritatively about the blues with a slight lisp. His name was Brian Jones.[3] He wanted to play the Delta-style slide guitar in Korner's band.

On March 17, 1962, Blues Incorporated would play in a new blues club in West London, Ealing. Shortly afterward Korner would receive a demo tape with three songs performed by a group from Dartford named Little Boy Blue and the Blue Boys. The tape was sent by a Mick Jagger. On the following Saturday

---

1 Philip Norman, *The Stones* (Harper, 2012), 12 f.

2 Ibid., 25.

3 Ibid., 27.

Mick would perform Chuck Berry's "Around and Around" with Korner's band. Korner noticed not so much the singing but the way the singer threw his hair around. After a moment of silence, there was a burst of applause for "someone whose love of blues could take him so far beyond the embarrassment barrier. The fact that he had copied Chuck Berry's phrasing note for note was further proof of being a true disciple."[4] Within a month, Mick had become Korner's second-string vocalist, an early sample of being bold. Even if you plan to promote a noble musical cause, an erotically charged movement can be the best service to gain traction for your cause. In the recent *Olé Olé* movie on the South American tour, Mick reveals a family tradition from childhood: to impersonate someone in a sketch on stage. There was no hiding—it was good training.

On April 7, 1962, Elmo Lewis, also known as Brian Jones, played Elmore James's "Dust My Blues" with blues band P.P. Pond in Korner's Ealing club. Mick and Keith were in the audience. "On Keith especially, the effect was instant hero worship."[5] As we know from etiquette books, it is the first impression that counts most. However, the worshipping was not a unilateral occurrence but led to mutual respect and know-how sharing. In subsequent conversations Keith would make blues jazz–oriented Brian discover Chuck Berry and Jimmy Reed. Brian quit P.P. Pond and started to recruit musicians for his own band. The first recruit was Ian Stewart. Thickset and muscular, with a long, pugnacious jaw, he looked anything but the blues pianist he claimed to be.[6] Stew had a steady daytime job as a shipping clerk with Imperial Chemical Industries in Buckingham Gates. When Mick and Keith joined the band, Ian thought they were going to starve together. During practice sessions at the Bricklayer's Arms, Brian and Keith would spontaneously develop a novel style of guitar interaction. "They would play, not as lead and subordinate rhythm, but as a duet," which led to the first-ever "two-guitar band,"[7] a first but impactful innovation. The proposition of a two-guitar band is particularly interesting. It is one of the key differentiators of the Stones, and it is enriched through the stylistic complementarity of the two guitarists. Brian was the blues purist and Keith the Chuck Berry fan. As he once put it, he built an entire career on a single riff. It was musically helpful that the two musicians came from different schools and enriched each other as well as the rest of the band. How boring it

---

4 Ibid., 31.
5 Ibid., 39.
6 Ibid., 40.
7 Ibid., 41.

would have been if both had played exactly the same style. Complementarity beats cloning; but the vision had to be shared. Furthermore, the two-guitar concept further evolved over the years. Initially, it simply meant that there was no work allocation along the lead guitar/rhythm guitar lines. Later, during the 1978–1981 period you can see in concert videos that distinctive riff modules of particular songs such as "Shattered" fluctuate from Keith to Ron and back between tours, concerts, and even while playing a track.

In summer 1962 the BBC offered Korner's Blues Incorporated its first nationwide broadcast but offered to pay for only four musicians. Korner shed the most dispensable band member, the vocalist. So much for Mick being the center of the world. Luckily Mick mastered his ego and sacrificed his vanity for the greater good. He did not mind being dropped if it helped to bring blues to a national audience. A temporary sacrifice that proved fruitful for later reward. As the broadcast clashed with Korner's regular Thursday booking at the Marquee, Korner was replaced there by his original Ealing vocalist Long John Baldry but offered the Bricklayers Arms boys a chance to produce themselves as an intermission band. On July 12, six future Rolling Stones faced their first audience. "Before we'd played a note, we could feel the hostility" (Dick Taylor).[8] Two days before the French Bastille Day, we can thankfully celebrate the Rolling Stones Day. Those starting the French Revolution in 1798 faced the hostility of a century-old system fiercely defending its privileges. The emerging Stones faced a less threatening form of resistance from their audience: they did not meet their listening expectations (in return, their revolution was more peaceful than the French Revolution). In fact, not meeting expectations can kill an act before it has really started. It takes courage to impose your proposition against resistance before you have established yourself on a market, but in this case, it paid off. It also reflects another important factor: while the young Stones may have sought wealth, sex, and fame from the very beginning, they were not willing to compromise their artistic vision; they had set out to confess the Afro-American blues. In other words, they had a musical project that was driven by passion rather than commerciality.

2. *Taking off*

Not every lasting success is based on a detailed long-term business plan. In October 1962, the most pressing question for the Rolling Stones was whether

---

8 Ibid., 43.

they could survive another week. Harold Pendleton, the jazz-oriented Marquee manager who disapproved of the Stones' music, would only offer them replacement slots. In a long letter to *Jazz News*, Brian complained about the "pseudo-intellectual snobbery" of the jazz scene. He was right to stick to the band's vision. However, what they lacked indeed was a drummer, the ultimate sign of professionalism. All the drummers they tried to recruit were from jazz bands and unable or unwilling to find the rhythm and blues backbeat, except Charlie Watts. But Charlie had a steady and well-paying job as a graphic designer in an advertising agency. "We were all a bit in awe of Charlie then. ... We thought he was much too expensive for us" (Keith).[9]

Brian, Mick, and Keith rented a squalid two-room flat in a shabby house in Edith Grove, Chelsea, with "damp and peeling wallpaper, grubby furniture, filthy curtains and naked light bulbs that functioned at the behest of a single, iron-clad electric coin meter." Keith, jobless and penniless, spent most of his days in the flat. After Brian had lost his job, he would do so as well, and both would practice their guitar play. Not getting dates in the Marquee or even Gomelsky's Piccadilly Club, the Stones set out to start a club of their own. Initially, Ian drove them in his van to clubs in Sutton, Richmond, Putney, and Twickenham. If there was no piano in the club, Ian would sleep in the van. There was still no permanent drummer. Around Christmas, bass player Dick Taylor announced his departure, another setback. However, no business can be allowed to depend on one single individual, and virtually every departure can be overcome. Bill Wyman, a working-class (origin) semiprofessional bass player with the Cliftons, went to audition with the much younger Stones only to find them "off-puttingly 'bohemian' and 'arty.'"[10] The Stones were impressed by the size of Bill's equipment, a Vox 850.

During the winter of 1962–1963, one of the worst in a century, and although the water pipes at Edith Grove were all frozen, Brian managed to wash his hair every day. The diet was mainly potatoes and eggs. The Stones listened to the blues records they had imported from America over and over again until they were able to copy every single note. It was "Benedictine work" (Keith). Brian mentally and financially abused one of his simple-minded admirers, Dick Hattrell, and made him hand over his army greatcoat and money. "He would obediently follow them to their local hamburger bar, hand them more money and, at Brian's command, stand patiently in the snow until they came

---

9 Ibid., 45.
10 Ibid., 50.

out again."[11] In January 1963, appearances of the Beatles in the Saturday night TV pop show *Thank Your Lucky Stars* and in the BBC's *Saturday Club* set off the Beatles mania. The Stones listened from under the blankets at Edith Grove. When Brian wrote a letter to the BBC, they were given an audition. The feedback was that "they liked us as a group but they couldn't book us because 'the singer sounds too colored'" (Bill).[12] Another blow to Mick's vanity. Luckily, no short-term thinking manager was around then to sack him on the spot. When drummer Tony Chapman left, Charlie reluctantly agreed to join.

A foreign element proved helpful. Giorgio Gomelsky, a Russian émigré exiled from Georgia to Switzerland and educated in Italy and Germany, had helped Chris Barber to set up the National Jazz League. The Stones had played in his Piccadilly Club, but Giorgio found their playing abominable. After the closure of the club, Giorgio found a new venue in the backroom of the Station Hotel in Kew Road, Richmond, named the Crawdaddy after the Bo Diddley song "Doing the Crawdaddy." Its first resident attraction for the Sunday night shows (7:00 to 10:30 p.m.) was the Dave Hunt Group featuring Ray Davies (later with the Kinks), a band that played in Louis Jordan's 1940s jump band style. When the group could not make one gig, due to snow, Giorgio rang up Ian Stewart. "Tell everyone in the band you guys are on next Sunday."[13] That first night the attendance was so much reduced that Giorgio went through the surrounding pubs offering half-price tickets. But within weeks the band had attracted a huge following, of which R&B enthusiasts were only the minor part; there were mods, rockers, art students, and middle-class youth. Initially, the crowd was merely standing and watching, until Giorgio's assistant Hamish Grimes "jumped on a tabletop and began to leap and flail his arms with the music like a dervish."[14] From that impromptu outburst evolved a twist-like dance peculiar to the Crawdaddy Club that could be performed by couples and singles alike. The 20-minute dancing frenzy became the ritual-like climax of each Stones session. From then on, Giorgio would give the band a lot of support, without ever trying to secure exclusivity as a manager. On the contrary, his advice was to let no one have control over them but themselves. A genuine business angel he was. While selfishness is inherent in human nature, it does not prevent many from tendering a helping hand. Being in contact with the

---

11 Ibid., 53.
12 Ibid., 54.
13 Ibid., 57.
14 Ibid., 59.

Beatles' Brian Epstein, he invited the Beatles to the Crawdaddy on a night when the Stones were performing. The Beatles were complimentary about the Stones' playing, in particular, John Lennon. ("You really play that harmonica, don't you?")[15] The Beatles, celebrities by then, liked to see a group like themselves before Epstein had cleaned up their music and appearance. The Stones in return recognized their R&B blood brothers who had traded Chuck Berry riffs against more commercial pop compositions. Mick was intrigued to learn that John and Paul had already written some hundred songs together and that they had a share in their own music-publishing company. Mick asked Paul how much one could earn per song in royalties. A week later, the Stones were invited to the Beatles' first major London concert, a Pop Prom run by the BBC at the Royal Albert Hall. After the concert, Brian would say to Giorgio, "That's what I want, Giorgio. *That's* what I want." (Emphasis in original)[16] None of the Stones had songwriting ambitions; they just wanted to cover blues songs. However, when prompted to write for commercial reasons, Mick and Keith proved to be surprisingly good at it. They were good at it as a team. As Mick's and Keith's later respective solo efforts would reveal, none was individually as good as a songwriter as they were together. The key factor that distinguishes the Stones from the Beatles is that Mick and Keith were interdependent. They really needed each other to come up with a song, whereas John and Paul each penned their own songs effortlessly. In the long run, the unfolding awareness about their interdependency helped them to overcome the inevitable tensions that come with any long-term collaboration and which led to the breaking up of the Beatles after only a few years. Unfortunately, not being gifted for songwriting would turn out to be the main factor in Brian gradually losing band leadership, influence, and power to the emerging Jagger–Richard duo and eventually fading away from the band due to increased drug addiction.

One of Ian's friends, Glyn Johns, worked at IBC Studios in Portland Place. Glyn, another helping hand on the Stones' path, was allowed to record artists he thought promising. In one evening, the Stones recorded four songs, including Chuck Berry's "Come On." But while the Beatles had their second number one single, the Stones were still searching for record company access.

Nineteen-year-old Andrew Loog Oldham, the son of a Dutch American air force officer killed in a mission over Germany, was in search of glamor and fame. A PR assignment for American record producer Phil Spector altered

---

15 Ibid., 61.
16 Ibid., 62.

his conception of the music business. Phil Spector was the first producer to be as famous as his performing acts. From then on Andrew wanted to become another Phil. In April 1963, Andrew went to see the Stones at the Crawdaddy. Giorgio was in Switzerland burying his father, and that night the club atmosphere was morbid. The Stones would do their blues roots thing, sitting on a ring of bar stools in a morbid atmosphere. He intuitively felt their potential. However, he knew he was not able to manage a pop group on his own; he went to see Brian Epstein and proposed a deal whereby Epstein could have 50 percent of the Rolling Stones. Epstein felt he was too busy and declined. Andrew, showing perseverance, was luckier with music agent Eric Easton. Both went to see the Stones at the Crawdaddy. Andrew was not familiar with the sound and songs of R&B. However, intuitively he felt, "The Rollin' Stones were six who became one."[17] He also felt the particularity of Mick's voice: "It wasn't just a voice. … It was an instrument, a declaration, not backed by a band, but a part of the band, their decree."[18] Easton on the other hand was skeptical. Andrew walked up to Charlie and asked who their leader was. Charlie pointed to Brian who immediately ensured Andrew would not talk to Mick or Keith. "Brian was a really weird shape with that big head, broad body and short legs, like a Welsh pony. But he had incredible magnetism. He could make you focus on just his face" (Andrew).[19] While Easton pondered strategy, Andrew tried to create intimacy with the Stones, pretending to share their mission to bring pure blues and R&B to a wider audience. When Giorgio returned from Switzerland, the Stones, represented by Brian, had signed a three-year exclusive management contract with Andrew and Easton. A side letter to the agreement secured another £5 per week to Brian.[20] Giorgio, the helping hand, was out of the picture.

Dick Rowe of Decca Records was known as the man who turned the Beatles down. His sole consolation was that no pop group would last longer than six months. Now he was looking for the next Beatles up in the North, attending a talent show in Liverpool's Philharmonic Hall. The jury member next to him, George Harrison, remarked that there was a group down in London he should consider. When George turned his head around, Rowe had already left. Rowe watched the Stones in the Crawdaddy, but following protocol, he tried to find

17 Andrew Oldham, *Stoned* (Vintage, 2001), 188.

18 Ibid., 189.

19 Norman, *Stones*, 72.

20 Ibid., 73.

out who was managing them by calling around his usual contacts. Nobody had ever heard of the Stones, but eventually someone said, "Try Eric Easton."[21] A deal was made within days, but a problem remained: the five songs recorded at IBC were still held by IBC and could be viewed as a prior recording commitment. Easton advised the Stones to approach IBC, say they had split up but wanted to buy the tape back as a souvenir. Unsuspecting IBC sold the tape at a cost of £109.

Easton and Rowe concluded a two-year recording contract, and Rowe wanted to show gratitude. While the Beatles, after many rejections, had to accept miserable conditions offered by EMI (a royalty of one penny per double-sided record, with an annual increment of one farthing), Rowe generously offered the standard record royalty rate, that is, 5 percent of the retail price of each copy sold. With the deal being done, Rowe proposed recording dates in the Decca studios and talented Decca producers to supervise the recording. Juvenile Andrew retorted that the Stones would not use the Decca studios and already had a producer: himself.[22] Andrew followed Phil Spector's advice that all material taped in the studios of a record company remained that company's copyright. By recording the Stones independently, then leasing the record masters back to Decca for manufacture and distribution, Oldham would retain copyright and control over what was recorded.[23] This was the first such deal in Great Britain. Decca was so desperate that the proposal was accepted.[24] Andrew rented the Olympics studio for £5 an hour and rushed the Stones into recording their first single: the Berry cover "Come On." The price of engineering services being included in the hourly rate, Andrew told the engineer to mix the recording overnight. He would pick it up the next morning. As Decca recording artists, the Stones had now entered into a new galaxy.

Andrew suggested that the independent recording company be called Impact Sound. Impact Sound would take 25 percent of all revenues and in return assumed payment for recording sessions, time, trouble, and investment. The remaining 75 percent were for the Stones, three times more than the classic recording royalties. Andrew would later find out that Impact Sound was

---

21 Ibid., 76.
22 Ibid., 77.
23 Oldham, *Stoned*, 204.
24 Norman, *Stones*, 77.

registered in the name of Eric Easton Ltd.[25] Like in any economic sector, the music industry has people who put themselves first.

Easton was anxious that the Stones should pass BBC muster. He suggested to Andrew that they might have to sack Mick Jagger. Easton had already discussed with Brian that nothing should be allowed to get in the way of this great opportunity, including Mick. Ian, who overheard the conversation, reported that Brian agreed with Easton that Jagger had always had a weak voice and "has to be careful if he wants to sing night after night, we'll just have to get rid of him if necessary." The third attempt at emasculating Mick. Luckily, it remained without consequences. Luckily indeed, because managers did have the power to expel band members, even if they were Mick Jagger.

Sir Edward Lewis, Decca's chairman, did not believe in publicity. Hence there was no Decca support for the launch of the recording. For Decca, the Stones was just another band. Not surprisingly, press feedback on the recordings was less than enthusiastic, except for a full-page article in the *Daily Mirror*, written by Patrick Doncaster, a friend of Giorgio, the helping hand. The single satisfied neither blues nor pop purists; it fell between all chairs. Andrew knew he had to secure an appearance in *Thank Your Lucky Stars*. To get a booking to mime their record, the Stones had to conform to the Beatles pop group pattern and wear matching suits. Andrew also decided to drop Ian from the stage lineup. Six were too many, and Ian looked too normal. As delicately as such painful decisions are communicated to those concerned, Ian would find out by discovering that there was no stage suit for him. Brian reassured him sincerely or with crocodile tears: "You're still a full member of the group, Stew. You'll still get a sixth share, I promise you."[26] How many corporate managers recur every day to this type of undignified rhetoric? In fact, Ian was allowed to stay on as road manager and backup pianist, and he did. Ian's pride was badly hurt, but he accepted the support role in lieu of equity partnership. It is noteworthy that in this support role, Ian proved extremely influential. Taking loyalty to the extreme, he would ensure that the Stones play no (or very few) minor chords while on stage. He also contributed his very unique skills as boogie pianist to many of the band's albums up to the day he died.

Despite the mitigating success in the charts, Easton sent the Stones on a nationwide tour of nonstop one-nighters through the town halls and ballrooms of Whittlesey, Soham, Wisbech, and the like, headed by the American Everly

---

25 Oldham, *Stoned*, 205.

26 Norman, *Stones*, 81.

Brothers and featuring Stones hero Bo Diddley. For Andrew, the Stones rose to the occasion: "Every night the band learned new tricks from the more accomplished performers they played alongside."[27] Touring was physically and emotionally tough (32 days, 2 shows per day, and 3 days of rest). "It was the road that brought out and hardened their toughness."[28] Somewhere on tour, Charlie was the first Stone to abandon his stage suit.[29] Who would have expected that sign of rebellion from Charlie? For most of the tour, Brian managed to stay in slightly more expensive hotels than the others.

In October 1963, the Beatles made another TV appearance in *Sunday Night at the London Palladium* with an audience of 15 million watchers. While Andrew was walking through the streets of Soho, desperately searching for a follow-up single, John and Paul jumped out of a taxi. "'Ello, Andy. You're looking unhappy. What's the matter?"—"Oh, I'm fed up. The Stones can't find a song to record."—"Oh, we've got a song we've almost written. The Stones can record that if yer like."[30] John and Paul went to Studio 51 with Andrew, and the Stones were waiting while John and Paul finished their song. It only took two hours at Kingsway Sound Studios, Holborn, to record "I Wanna Be Your Man" in pure Chicago blues style. Media feedback was, again, weak. NME wrote just one line: "The latest group to try their chart luck with a Lennon & McCartney song."[31] For the B-side the Stones hastily taped a 12-bar blues instrumental that counted as an original composition.

On January 6, 1964, the Stones were sent on tour again, now big enough to merit equal top billing with Phil Spector's Ronettes. The show attracted media attention for its vocal volume and body action. On January 17, Decca released an EP with a handful of songs for extracting additional mileage from their act, which went into the Top Ten Singles chart one week after its release. After the tour, Robert Stigwood confessed that he had gone bankrupt while the tour was on and thus could not pay the agreed £16,000. Keith roughed him up at the Scotch of St James club.

When Bill returned home to his new house in Farnborough after many consecutive weeks of touring, his dog took him for a burglar and bit him. Mick, Keith, and Brian had left the Edith Grove flat, and Mick and Keith were now

---

27 Oldham, *Stoned*, 240.

28 Ibid., 239.

29 Norman, *Stones*, 86.

30 Ibid., 90.

31 Cited after Oldham, *Stoned*, 240.

sharing a flat with Andrew in Willesden, North London. People noted that Andrew's management style was revolutionary. He lived with the act. "The whole PR thing he did with the Stones was very novel, it was new" (Lionel Bart).[32] While the Beatles were conquering America and were watched by 70 million viewers on the *Ed Sullivan Show*, Andrew developed the image of the Stones as dirty and ugly, culminating in the *Melody Maker* headline "WOULD YOU LET YOUR DAUGHTER MARRY A STONE?" John Lennon, who suffered from Epstein's image strategy, believed that Andrew had hijacked the original Beatles image for the Stones.[33]

Brian was now living in considerably greater comfort at his pregnant girlfriend's parents' but moved to a smaller flat in Chester Street, Belgravia, after their breakup. When the mother of the newborn visited Brian in his flat, neighbors would hear bumps and crashes through the ceiling. Brian enjoyed his renown as a pop star, with its dose of fame, attention, mobbing, clothes, money, girls, shopping, and night clubs. He would spend large amounts on shirts and jackets, and what he did not buy he would "cheerfully steal."[34] On tour, Brian would eat Keith's portion of chicken, no other food being available that night. Brian continued to regard himself as leader of the band and, as such, felt entitled to extra pay and comfort, not knowing that the others were aware of his secret deals. On the other hand, his musicianship continued to give strength to the Stones. Being unable to write songs, he was talented in dabbling different instruments and contributed as a colorist to the increasingly psychedelic band sound.

For their third single, the Stones would turn Buddy Holly's mild and reflective "Not Fade Away" into a rough if not wild piece of rhythm and blues. However, the Stones were tired, worn out by fatigue, not getting along with each other, and showing the strain of five months on the road. Andrew called Gene Pitney for help; Decca was crying for the follow-up release, but not only would the Stones not sing together, but they were not even talking to each other. Gene took a bottle of cognac and went to the studio, pretending it was his birthday. Recorded at Regent Sound after studio employees had left for the evening, the song was taped at the culmination of a drunken studio party including Andrew, Phil Spector, Freddy Bienstock, two members of the

---

32 Ibid., 296.
33 Ibid., 294.
34 Norman, *Stones*, 104.

Hollies, and Gene.[35] As the Stones had only come with one song, they needed a B-side. It took Mick and Phil 10 minutes to cough up some lyrics and 20 more minutes to capture them on tape, over a simple 12-bar blues structure, "Little By Little." "The Rolling Stones finally knew how to make hit records. They were self-contained." Gene remembers: "It was one of those days where the Stones all hated each other. ... [Andrew] had the nice ability to get them to put things out in the studio. Left to their own egos, they always had problems with each other."[36] The single quickly reached top five status: quite a result. Andrew had identified those record shops that reported sales to the radio stations. A genius in marketing strategy, he would send out a small armada of teenage girls to buy all stocks on the release day and return to the same shops on the day after. The shops were still out of stock but would place new orders, which they reported to the radio station. Andrew called his shoppers off the retail run as soon as the single reached position 38. The single continued to climb on its own, totaling 250,000 sales.

The necessity of producing material for a first LP caused Andrew to lock up Keith and Mick in their kitchen until they had composed their first song. Only one Jagger–Richard song was deemed good enough for the album; the remainder were R&B covers. Andrew would get 35 tracks together, ring the music publishers, and say, "Give me 15 per cent of the song, or it's not going on the album."[37] The album cover was inspired by the Beatles' *With the Beatles*, but Oldham insisted that there was no group name or album title printed on the cover, nothing but a picture. Andrew's sleeve notes on the back started with the famous words "The Rolling Stones are more than a group. They are a way of life." By the day of its release on April 16, 1964, the album had sold 100,000 copies in advance orders, compared to 6,000 for the Beatles' debut album. Andrew boasted that the Stones had knocked the Beatles' second album off its chart position (true but it had been in the charts since November 1963).

Writing songs meant to enter into the new and lucrative business of music publishing and earning higher royalties. With the "advent of the piano as a piece of furniture," audiences leaving vaudevilles were able to take home sheet music. Sheet music was also sold to local bands and ballroom band leaders. Publishing evolved to promoting live radio performances. "The Beatles, with their growing catalogue of original songs, helped to create an important new

35 Ibid., 95.
36 Oldham, *Stoned*, 286.
37 Ibid., 268.

revenue stream." Whenever a song was played, the publisher collected a roy-alty and kept 50 percent of it.[38] However, Andrew was not purely altruistic in his efforts. He wanted Mick and Keith to write songs that Andrew "wanna be Phil Spector" would produce with other acts of his choice. The most famous publishers of that day were Freddy Bienstock and David Platz, who had set up Essex Music. Andrew and the Stones formed their own two publishing entities, Mirage Music Ltd and Nanker Phelge Music Ltd, and assigned the administra-tion rights to Essex Music. For Tony Calder, "the deals the Stones got on paper were absolutely sensational—they had the greatest deals, fair to this day."[39]

Andrew explains,

> A song has many potential sources of income: sheet music, the pennies paid every time you hear a song on the radio, the "mechanical royalties" paid to the writer and publisher for the use of the song each time a recording is sold. It all adds up, and if you have a national anthem, you are talking a lot of money; even a minor hit is going to put food on your table. In the old world a pound would come in, the publisher would take 10 or 15 per cent off the top for collecting the money, and "administrative charge." The remain-ing 90 per cent or so would be divided up 50/50 between the writers and publisher. So the publisher's total take would come to 60-65 per cent of the income. ... The publisher was indeed doing the writer a favor by agreeing to publish and represent his work; the publisher had all the contacts and all the data on which A&R man was looking for what kind of song for which act. Without a publisher and his connections, no song—no matter how commercial—would ever get recorded. ... We were past the stage where we needed a publisher to get us recordings; I just needed one to collect. Many publishers were loath to say goodbye to the good old days and the lion's share of the money. Platz seemed forward-thinking and ready to play it my way. He and Essex Music would get 15 per cent off the top for collect-ing, the rest being divided between Mick and Keith or the group as writers and the two publishing companies we had formed to cover both events.[40]

With Mick and Keith becoming a songwriter team, Brian started to feel left out. Brian did have songwriting ambitions but was too scared to put his songs

---

38 Ibid., 252.
39 Ibid., 258.
40 Ibid., 261.

forward.[41] Andrew "realised that Brian did not love pop music, therefore he could not write it. … Writing songs means one must pay attention to life, and Brian was loath to pay attention to anything but himself."[42] On the one hand, he wanted to duplicate the Beatles' superstardom, but on the other, he remained a blues purist and obstructed the others' efforts to reach the widest possible audience. For Andrew, Brian "resisted the symbiosis demanded by the group lifestyle, and so life was becoming a little more desperate for him day by day."[43]

In June 1964, the Stones took off to America, where they would be launched not as R&B iconoclasts but as "England's Newest Hitmakers," exploiting the craze for British pop. Dean Martin would make fun of them on his *Hollywood Palace* TV show. On the advice of Phil Spector, Andrew would book a session at RCA's Hollywood studio and later in Chicago at Chess Records, where their blues masters had all recorded.[44] Here, the Stones would record in the occasional presence of Muddy Waters their first number one hit, a cover of Bobby Womack's "It's All Over Now," one of their truly most accomplished recordings, full of awe still to listeners today, that contained the DNA of future hits to come. Eventually, unlike the Beatles, the Stones became used to recording during tours, which also exposed them to different studio and recording technologies.[45] In Texas, the Stones would meet saxophone virtuoso Bobby Keys. He would play the vast majority of great sax solos on the Stones' classic albums between 1969 and 1973 and remained part of the Stones' touring family until his death in 2014. The tour was a series of randomly scheduled one-night stands, mostly not well attended. "We couldn't see it at the time, but all that was really doing us some good. … America, that first tour really made us work. We had to fill up the spaces somehow."

By locking Mick and Keith into their kitchen until they had come up with a song, Andrew forced the boys to leave their comfort zone and surpass themselves. It worked. With Mick and Keith becoming confident in their ability to write songs like Lennon and McCartney, they laid another founding stone to their long-lasting career. At the level of conscious decision making, the monetary aspect may have been predominant, but the possibly unintended side

---

41 Ibid., 287.

42 Ibid., 288.

43 Ibid.

44 Norman, *Stones*, 112.

45 Sean Egan, ed., *The Mammoth Book of the Rolling Stones* (Robinson, 2013), 33.

effect was to create a musical legacy. The Stones tours over the years were never nostalgic, always a mix of new material and old material, frequently revisited. While the Stones give their songs different spins from tour to tour (e.g., "Under My Thumb": exotic and jazzy on *Aftermath*, punky and upbeat on *Got Live If You Want It!*, melancholic in minor during the 1969 US tour, and fat and pompous during the 1981 tour), their fundamental structure remains unchanged; it is cast in stone.

But there is another twist to the motivation behind songwriting. Andrew was not only, and maybe not even primarily, interested in the Stones' songwriting for *their* financial benefit but also for his *own*. He thought he could employ Mick and Keith as permanent songwriters for his Andrew Oldham Orchestra, a symphonic exercise in the best Phil Spector tradition, and some of its production can be found on CD or streaming services today. Admittedly it is very good stuff, a bit like James Last, but it has nothing to do with rock 'n' roll, blues, or the Stones as we know them today. There is, however, one highly intriguing by-product of that strategy: the first part of the album *Metamorphosis*, which was released in 1975 by Allen Klein without the band's consent. The cover showed the Stones as insects taking off their face masks, more than an allusion to Franz Kafka's Gregor Samsa. While critics and the Stones themselves have bashed the compilation, it is in fact a great and somewhat unusual listening experience. The B-side of the album consisted of studio outtakes from the 1968 to 1969 period, mature and dark, and the A-side was a classic Oldham product: really beautiful songs penned by Jagger/Richards, performed by Mick, backed up by a full-fledged symphony orchestra with strings, violins, Spanish guitars, trumpets, trombones, bells, and triangles. The songs are nice to listen to and prefigure popular albums like *Symphonic Elvis* and the like. Sometimes, a not so noble intent can end in adorable results.

In fact, as confirmed by recent documentaries, the Mick–Keith songwriting team was the beginning of Brian's end. It was from then on that he questioned his role in the band he had founded and led. It was a question to which he found no answer, except that his frustration pushed him to venture into "coloring" by playing exotic instruments to enrich the music's sound, a panic reaction with beautiful results. One of many examples of a business founder being bypassed by his creation and ultimately being pushed out by a new power-grabbing leadership with the stated ambition to take the venture to the "next level."

This being said, nothing suggests that Mick and Keith intentionally excluded Brian from being part of the songwriting. He just was not able to do it, and that was the result not only of his egocentricity, observed by Andrew, which made him obsessed with himself, but also, as confirmed by others, of his lack of self-confidence. He was so convinced of not being able to write a good song that he became the victim of his own belief. A good executive coach like my wife Sabine may have helped.[46] Or a partner in crime. As the later solo recording efforts of Mick and Keith reveal, neither of them can do great songs alone. Mick needs Dave Stewart to create songs, and Keith needs Steve Jordan. There is no obligation to be perfect on all fronts, but not drawing the right conclusions from a lucid self-analysis has a price.

3. *Flying on Autopilot*

The following three years would see the Stones propelled to stardom, evolving socially in the bohemian and art scene of swinging London through friendships with high society starlets such as Marianne Faithfull and Anita Pallenberg, becoming icons and being idolized like modern gods. Artistically, they were in search of a style. Andrew would push them to frequently release new albums on both sides of the Atlantic following different editorial policies: a mix of pop and R&B tracks with frequently suboptimal song material lacking consistency in musical policy. Note that there were general distinctions in album publication: in the United Kingdom, singles were not necessarily included on an album, whereas in the United States they were. However, this fact alone does not explain all of Andrews's editorial choices.

Andrew would pursue his branding efforts through his infamous back cover liner notes that caused uproar and scandal in the media. ("This is THE STONES' new disc within. Cast deep in your pockets for loot to buy this disc of groovies and fancy words. If you don't have the bread, see that blind man, knock him on the head, steal his wallet and low and behold, you have the loot.") A Conservative Member of the House of Lords would ask the director of public prosecutions to investigate this "deliberate incitement to criminal action." First attempts by Andrew to launch the Stones in the movie business, following on the Beatles' path, remained fruitless, but it reflected his strategy to engage in diversification of the brand and catch attention on several fronts of the pop culture.

Their second tour to America in October 1964 was a total success. On the famous TAMI show they performed next to James Brown, Chuck Berry, and the Beach Boys. Again, they recorded a few numbers in the RCA Hollywood

---

46 https://www.linkedin.com/in/sabine-baer-67245317/?originalSubdomain=be.

studios that would appear on a series of LPs to be released. In 1965, tours took them to Australia, Scandinavia, and France. In May of that year, a muse would inspire "Satisfaction" during Keith's sleep in Clearwater, Florida. The Stones rushed to the Chess studios in Chicago, but the usual magic did not work this time—the result sounded folksy.[47] It was only in the RCA Hollywood studio with David Hassinger's engineering that the production came together (interestingly, Keith was still not satisfied with the final take used for release). Reportedly, Brian hated the song so much that during concerts he would play "Popeye the Sailor Man" as its countermelody, which led to the first rumors about sacking him.[48] This was soon followed by "Get off of My Cloud" and other best-selling top hits. "It's difficult to realize what pressure we were under to keep on turning out hits. Each single you made in those days had to be better and do better. If the next one didn't do as well as the last one, everyone told you you were sliding out" (Keith).[49]

By then Andrew had "definitively cast himself as the sixth Stones—if not the first."[50] He had achieved much, and so had the Stones, but they were far from being millionaires. Keith still earned £50 a week. Decca would simply not pay out the royalties due until one year later. Their tours failed to make money. In order to remedy this situation, in July 1965, Andrew would have breakfast with a New York accountant, Allen Klein, also manager of Sam Cooke. Their dialogue went "Andrew, how'd you like to be a millionaire?"— "Very much" was the reply. "Okay, whaddaya want for now?"—"I want a Rolls-Royce."—"You got it."[51]

Allen Klein was born in 1932 in Newark, son of a kosher butcher. After his mother's early death, the father would put him and his sister into the Hebrew Shelter Orphanage. Allen Klein studied to become an accountant, and he was known for his enormous working capacity. Allen "specialised in obtaining large advance payments for recording artists."[52] When taking on teenage pop singer Buddy Knox, Allen discovered that his record company had withheld significant amounts of royalties. He managed to obtain them for his client. Allen's pitch was straightforward: "I can find you money you never knew

---

47 Philip Norman, *Mick Jagger* (Harper, 2013), 174.
48 Christopher Sandford, *The Rolling Stones—Fifty Years* (Simon & Schuster, 2013), 86.
49 Norman, *Stones*, 160.
50 Ibid., 140.
51 Ibid., 142.
52 Norman, *Jagger*, 182.

you even had." His technique was to harass the record company with an avalanche of legal writs. "If a corporation is big, it *has* to make mistakes." After unsuccessful career attempts in the movie business, Allen concentrated on the pop music industry. In 1964, Allen approached the Beatles' Brian Epstein to propose Klein's Sam Cooke as opening act. He also proposed to Epstein to manage the Beatles' finances. Epstein declined. He was more successful with Mickie Most, the Animals, Herman's Hermits and Donovan. The day after meeting Andrew, he met with Mick and Keith. While Mick found Allen somewhat repugnant, Allen deployed a "mastery of percentages and high-multiple mental arithmetic that held the former economics student transfixed."[53] He also impressed the other Stones, and a deal was made. Klein would take over the financial side; Andrew kept the creative parts of his job. Eric Easton was quickly dismissed and took legal action against Andrew and Allen. The Stones' affairs were transferred to Klein's London accountants, Goodman Myers. Andrew received his Rolls-Royce.

The timing was perfect. The two-year contract with Decca had expired and was still under renegotiation. Decca proposed 24 percent of the wholesale price or 4pence per record sold. Klein offered to intervene. He insisted on talking to no one else but Decca chairman Sir Edward Lewis. He took the Stones along, warning them not to speak a word. In the meeting, Decca agreed to pay the Stones $1.25 million in advance royalties, the largest advance payment ever in the music industry. Other sources mention advance royalties of £1 million for UK and international rights, plus £1.8 million for American rights.[54] The money was to be paid by Decca's US subsidiary into the Stones' collective company, Nanker Phelge Music. Allen would retain 20 percent, the double of the usual commission. Klein also hired a new booking agent, Tito Burns, and the Stones were to make five feature films to be financed by Decca. The first film was entitled *Only Lovers Left Alive*. The Stones, with the exception of Mick, followed the Beatles' precedent and invested in country houses.

In autumn 1965, the Stones would do their fourth and very exhausting US tour, alluded to in "19th Nervous Breakdown," one of a series of pills/mental breakdown songs. Allen liked doing things on a big scale. For the autumn 1965 US tour, he promised the Stones their own private aircraft. The reality was not that glamorous. The Stones traveled in a twin-propeller not a luxury

53 Ibid., 183.
54 Victor Bockris, *Keith* (Omnibus Press, 2013), 74.

jet. During one of Ken Kesey's Acid Test parties, Keith and Brian were initi-
ated to LSD.

During the next European tour, Burns was puzzled by Klein's instruction
to receive all concert earnings in person and pay them not into the Stones'
English bank account held by British publishing company Nanker Phelge
Music but into a Delaware company named Nanker Phelge USA. Klein
explained this was necessary to escape the British tax system. He failed to
mention that the Delaware company was in his name,[55] a small detail that he
must have conveniently forgotten—maybe he thought that it was not an issue.

In summer 1966, the Stones released *Aftermath*, their first album with only
own compositions. On this album, the Stones experimented with a variety
of styles and instruments including marimbas and recorders played by Brian
the "colorist." The album shocked the Anglo-Saxon world with its provocative
lyrics. It climbed to number two in the UK charts and would later be ranked
108 in Rolling Stone magazine's list of 500 greatest albums. Mick Jagger considered it retroactively as his favorite Stones album.

By the end of 1966, British society had realized that pop meant drugs.
Something had to be done. The Beatles, having received the MBE (Membership
of the Most Excellent Order of the British Empire), were no appropriate tar-
get for setting an example, despite John's "bigger than Jesus" gaffe. During a
weekend party at Keith's Redland, 19 police officers busted the place in search
of drugs. They found amphetamines. Charges were brought against Mick
and Keith. Mick could not travel to Monterey in the United States, where he
was supposed to co-organize with Paul McCartney and others the first flower
power festival as nonexecutive member of the festival's planning board. With
trial being imminent, there was no chance he would obtain a US immigration visa. The court hearing presided by 61-year-old Judge Leslie Block lasted
barely 30 minutes. The jury turned out a guilty verdict, and the court refused
bail. Handcuffed Mick was remanded in custody. The next day it was Keith's
turn. Mick received three months' imprisonment, and Keith received a full
year's imprisonment, with immediate effect. "I just went dead" (Mick).[56] For
a first offender with a borderline offense, a fine with probation would have
been standard. Judge Leslie Block wanted to set an example. Mick was jailed
in Brixton Prison, and Keith was jailed in Wormwood Scrubs, a reminiscence
of Oscar Wilde.

---

55 Ibid., 75.
56 Norman, *Jagger*, 251.

The Stones' lawyers appealed, and their publicists lobbied behind the scenes. On appeal, the hearing was scheduled with unusual speed but only after the summer break. Instructions were given not to oppose bail if requested. Mick and Keith were released but not allowed to travel abroad. During the appeal hearing, Lord Justice Parker reminded Mick and Keith of the responsibility they bore. Mick's conviction was upheld but the prison sentence quashed. Keith got both conviction and sentence overturned. A nightmare had ended, at least for the time being.

Out of jail, the peace-seeking Stones recorded the flower power hymn "We Love You" (with John Lennon and Paul McCartney singing along), and more generally, the psychedelic trend of the times would attract them increasingly, fueled by the Beatles' phenomenal "Sgt. Pepper's" release that set new standards in recording sophistication. The Beatles released "Sgt. Pepper's" on June 1, 1967.

In August 1967, Mick and Marianne Faithfull joined the Beatles in a transcendental meditation initiation meeting with Maharishi Mahesh Yogi in Bangor, North Wales. News came from London announcing the death of Brian Epstein. While the Beatles followed their guru for quite some time, Mick stepped by quickly, following his usual caution.

After Epstein's death, the bands discussed "merger plans," whereby they would share offices, build a joint recording studio, and run a commercial enterprise. Mick registered the name "Mother Earth" for the record label.[57] The plan was quashed by Klein, who feared losing control. In today's antitrust jargon, this project may not have created a full merger, as the plan was not to integrate the members of the two bands into one stage act. However, the mere idea of the Beatles and Stones collaborating not only in the back office but also on the commercial front is extremely intriguing.

With a new generation of bands coming up and the Stones having already lasted longer than most other acts, Mick wanted the Stones to do their own "Sgt. Pepper's." Andrew refused. The Stones went on strike, repeatedly making Andrew wait for hours in the studio. Andrew understood the signs on the wall and quit. Rave magazine wrote, "Mick Jagger is out on his own, and he knows it. He has no acknowledged manager, no agent and no record producer. … He is the king Stone, the man in charge, whether he likes it or not."[58] The

---

57 Ibid., 273.
58 Ibid., 272.

Stones went on to choose their own angle at the mystic flower power movement and recorded *Their Satanic Majesties Request*, released in December 1967.

The biggest surprise was to find a song composed by Bill Wyman among the 10 tracks, "In Another Land." Bill had been the only Stone in the studio on time, and he used his chance. Later Mick and Keith worked on the track and agreed to put it on the album. Mick asked Bill for a share in the publishing rights. "Then the news that someone else in the band wrote songs was kept jealously under wraps. On the album credits it was attributed to 'the Rolling Stones'; only on its American release as a single did Bill get an individual credit."[59] However, while the Stones had turned out a number of fantastic single releases (mostly flowery ballads) during that period, and despite the album selling well, it did not convince the critics who benchmarked it against "Sgt. Pepper's." Andrew having been sacked, Mick and Keith themselves produced the album, which resulted in a less than optimal recording product. For some, it put the status of the Stones in jeopardy: "It is an identity crisis of the first order and one that will have to be resolved … if their music is to continue to grow" (Jon Landau).[60]

The story about Bill's songs and credits and the band's crediting policy is telling. The Beatles started with Lennon/McCartney, but when one or two of George's songs made it on the album, he was credited without any fuzz about it. The Stones' crediting system was tighter. The basis was the Jagger/Richards credit, and not only Bill but also Mick Taylor would later complain about the bottleneck created by the Glimmer Twins. On *Black and Blue*, released after Mick T.'s departure, the Glimmer Twins gave in partially, crediting Billy Preston and Ronnie Wood with having each "inspired" one song. Not sure this brings financial benefit, but it is at least a nice gesture to reward the contribution made. Curiously, disputes in later years about whether Keith is allowed to sing lead on one song or two on any album were not financially driven. Keith probably just wanted to personally sing a song particularly dear to him, and Mick may have been afraid of losing ground, since his status in the Stones was that of the lead singer and front man controlling the stage. In the late 1960s, some bands like Deep Purple deliberately credited all members on all or most songs, which was a statement about their more democratic constitutional mindset. In the case of Bill, the band leadership probably regretted its generosity and tried to claw back some of the credits, even if this meant wiping out the memory of the song's authorship.

Interpersonal dynamics in rock bands are not very different from those in other types of professional services firms, for example, in law firms or accounting firms. An alpha male remains an alpha male whatever the profession exercised, and some are just more driven and competitive than others. In her recent memoirs, Tina Turner describes Mick as being very competitive. When he was complimented on his good-looking hair, Mick retorted, "Yes, and it is mine."[61] More importantly, Tina describes Mick as *positively* competitive. In fact, society's views on competitiveness are split. Some view competitiveness as the expression of egoistic ruthlessness. Others see it as the necessary sting of vanity that drives humanity forward. In his extensive commentary of the Jewish Bible, Alsacian Rabbi Elie Munk explains that when God created the world, he intentionally instilled a zest of vanity in the human soul. If no one was jealous of his neighbor's car, the GDP would never grow. Being ambitious, competitive, and reasonably vain is not a character flaw but a condition for moving the world forward. Nor does it mean that competitiveness leads to egoism. In her wonderful memoirs, Tina Turner praises her longtime friendship with the Stones. They were there whenever she needed them (as was David Bowie).

The question thus is how we use our competitiveness. Shortly after the end of World War I, the French poet and philosopher Paul Valéry reflected about what had triggered the war. His answer is straightforward: fatigue. For Valéry, man is essentially competitive.[62] Competition includes rivalry and hostility, as such hostility is part of human nature. There may be ugly winners[63] and disappointed losers,[64] but competition remains a creative process as long as the actors are in good mental health and able to create. It is only when man feels exhausted that he will become destructive. Just like the toddler who builds

---

61 Tina Turner, *The Autobiography* (Century, 2018), 164.

62 Paul Valéry, *La Crise de l' Esprit, Première lettre*, 1919: "Et qu'est-ce que la paix? La paix est peut-être l'état de choses dans lequel l'hostilité naturelle des hommes entre eux se manifeste par des créations, au lieu de se traduire par des destructions comme fait la guerre. C'est le temps d'une *concurrence créatrice*, et de la lutte des productions. Mais moi, ne suis-je pas fatigué de produire ? N'ai-je pas épuisé le désir des tentatives extrêmes et n'ai -je pas abusé des savants mélanges ? Faut-il laisser de côté mes devoirs difficiles et mes ambitions transcendantes?" (emphasis mine).

63 Cf. The Rolling Stones, *Winning Ugly*, on: Dirty Work, 1986.

64 Cf. The Beatles, *I'm a Loser*, on: Beatles for Sale, 1964.

a Lego bridge and when caught by a moment of sudden frustration angrily destroys it with a brush.

The Stones must have managed to overcome their moments of fatigue over 60 years now, allowing them to remain competitively creative, which may be their biggest overall achievement. The creatively competitive relationship between Mick and Keith, which became more and more turbulent over the years, may even be the real reason behind the Stones' continued creative and financial success. Had one of them ousted the other, and be it out of personal insecurity, the Stones may have quickly turned into a deflated balloon.

The early Stones had equal shares in their company, which was an expression of basic fairness, but songwriting royalties come on top and provided extra income and status to those desiring, deserving, and controlling the credits. This created room and incentives for personal skills and ambition and reward for individual talent, and it also contributed to developing a hierarchy and pecking order, which is a necessity for any human organization to survive in the longer term. Athenian-style democracy is admirable on paper but unsustainable in practice, as endless debates distract attention and deviate essential resources from the creative and productive processes. A drummer other than Charlie may have been frustrated about not getting the same attention as the lead singer, but he may prefer to be the drummer in a successful band rather than the cashier in a supermarket. The challenge is to allow every band member to "find their place" in the wider organization, as Ian did. The same applies to the members of the touring family who accompany the Stones from the 1980s to our days.

The counterpart of pecking order must be basic fairness and mutual respect. As years go by, showing respect and paying dues to others within and outside the band becomes increasingly important in the Stones' conduct of operations. This is probably the greatest management success of the Stones compared to any other band. There is no "I, Me, Mine." The gradual acknowledgment of a "higher authority" contributed to this achievement. It took the Stones many years to realize this. In a first stage, they realized that the band, that is, "The Rolling Stones," is a distinct persona from its individual members, with a distinct identity of its own. The overall musical texture of the Rolling Stones is more edgy and energetic than that of the solo efforts of its members, and that applies to all solo efforts including the efforts of Mick, Keith, Ron, Bill, Charlie, and Mick T.

A separate band personality is comparable to the concept of a "legal person," an aggregation of tangible and intangible assets, including man power, that is recognized by law as a distinct person with distinct obligations and rights attached to it. In early trade, partnerships, companies, and corporations were used as a means of pooling resources and sharing risks. As legal historian Howard J. Berman explains in *Law and Revolution*, the legal concept of the legal person was developed in canonical law, which imputed such a distinct personality beyond the aggregation of its individual ministers to the church (ecclesia). But behind and above the church as a legal person and organization, there is the underlying idea of the church as a spiritual community with its own pneumatic space in which the community spirit can evolve. The Stones members eventually came to view the Rolling Stones as such a pneumatic individuality, as different interview statements made around the 50th band anniversary reflect. However, this does not have to translate in equal pay or status. When the Stones hired Darryl Jones to replace departed Bill, the question was whether he was just an additional touring support like Bernard Fowler and Lisa Fischer or whether he was a genuine member of the band. While Mick commented something like Darryl was joining too late to be a real Rolling Stone, Keith took the opposite view, stating that, for him, everyone who is on stage with the Rolling Stones is a member of the band, whatever the contractual arrangements say.

The consciousness of a distinct group personality was not the end of acknowledging a "higher authority." As brilliantly told in Victor Bockris's unrivaled biography of Keith (it tells you more about Keith than even Keith's *Life*), Keith had a spiritual awakening in the 1990s, that is, just after the Stones had overcome their biggest ever dispute and launched their second career that has lasted until today. Call it "resurrection." It was around that time that he started "paying dues" by recording gospel songs with a group of Jamaican reggae roots musicians, and he declared that whenever the Stones play outdoor, God is a member of the band. In the more recent tour documentary *Olé Olé* about their South American tour, the band members make many references about "having received" something, without specifying from whom, but suggesting that they were simply an instrument through which a message from higher up was passed through.

Coming back to Bill for a moment. He did have songwriting talents. In fact, he and future band member Ron seem to be the two Stones members who excel in writing good songs without other people's help. Keith needs Steve Jordan and Mick relies on David Stewart. But even fans of Bill, one of the greatest bass players of all times, will admit that his songs are of a different style than typical Stones material. They are well construed, nicely evolving pop songs, but they don't have that edge that is the essence of the Stones' sound. There is thus a question of strategic alignment and branding. It is not because a band plays music that it should play any type of music. Both artistically and commercially, there must be an identity which supports the brand. While inviting guest musicians and other colorists to add bandwidth, it is essential to keep focus on the main track. It is therefore understandable that independently of efforts to maintain the pecking order there was a certain artistically justified reluctance on Mick and Keith's part to put Bill's songs on the Stones albums. In Bill's case, this had consequences. While Charlie, Ron, and Ian were comfortable to fill in the roles assigned to them, Bill was not. Bill's frustration grew over the years. It led him to standing motionless onstage during concerts and looking intentionally bored, until he decided to quit in the early 1990s when he was in his mid-to-late 50s. He has been touring clubs since with a group of musician friends, doing what he really likes. Artistically it may not be as interesting as his work for the Stones. However, as a longtime group member Bill had made his lasting contribution to the world's cultural heritage and was therefore entitled to enjoy the remainder of his life in a nonexecutive way by doing what he enjoyed most.

Part Two—Turning Talent into Gold (1969–1988)

1. Men Overboard

Since the break with Andrew, the Stones had their management office in Maddox Street, close to Piccadilly. Mick hired Epstein's assistant Jo Bergman to run it with fan club secretary Shirley Arnold. Shirley remarked Mick's keenness with his new role as businessman and employer: "He loved coming in for boardroom meetings with lawyers and accountants."[65] There was an atmosphere of total efficiency, unlike in the Beatles' Apple company.

It was eight months since the Stones had toured America. The big question was, "Would they get visas despite their criminal records?" They took their chances and got on the plane. Upon arrival at JFK, they were thoroughly searched and warned about future entry refusals should they be caught with drugs again.

In 1968, Mick starred in Nicolas Roeg's rather dark gangster movie *Performance*, which had a rather decent budget of $1.1 million, of which $100,000 were for Mick. In parallel, the Stones worked on their musical comeback. The Stones hired a new producer, the young American Jimmy Miller who had worked for the Spencer Davis Group and was junior enough to accept a role that was rather technical. The comeback materialized immediately: with "Jumping Jack Flash," the "perfect antidote" to Majesties' "hippie wooziness" (Norman)[66] and the first song whose lyrics allowed Mick to create a character he could endorse. Inspired by the growing folk-rock movement, December 1968–released *Beggar's Banquet* was overall a rather acoustic album. Decca had opposed the original cover sleeve, a dirty toilet in front of a wall filled with obscene graffiti, causing a delay of several months in the album's release. French moviemaker Jean-Luc Godard filmed the recording of "Sympathy for the Devil" for his anti–Vietnam War movie *One Plus One*, but despite a touch of counterculture antiestablishment underground, "Street Fighting Man" posed the question in nuanced terms: "What can a poor boy do, except to sing for a rock 'n' roll band?"

At the same time, the Stones produced a Christmas special for BBC television, following the example of the Beatles' *Magical Mystery Tour* TV show broadcast a year previously. During 48 hours of uninterrupted filming, the Stones put together their *Rock and Roll Circus*, with guest acts such as John Lennon,

---

65 Norman, *Stones*, 282.
66 Norman, *Jagger*, 284.

Yoko Ono, Eric Clapton, Jimi Hendrix, Mitch Mitchell, Jethro Tull, and the Who. The Stones played at the end of the show, dressed-up in Hogwarts-style wizard clothes, but the show was never broadcasted. Mick had vetoed it—it seems that the vigorous Who had upstaged the tired Stones.

While the Stones had battled Decca over the album sleeve, Andrew and Eric Easton battled each other, and both battled Allen Klein over the $1.25 million advance royalties from Decca that Klein had artfully diverted to his Nanker Phelge USA company. After a year of litigation, Klein proposed Oldham to settle for one million dollars, buying off Oldham's residual interests in the Rolling Stones.

Klein's exit turned out to be a mixed blessing as he managed to walk away with the rights to all the songs of the Stones' early period up to and including "Brown Sugar" and "Wild Horses." This includes most of the great hits that are fit for radio play. To grow financially, the Stones had to write more radio-fit songs or to tour. This may also explain why the Stones put so much energy in developing tours as an artistic success and a vehicle to financial success.

In the early 1970s, Klein released a flurry of compilation albums that the Stones would moan about. They had catchy titles such as *Rock 'n' Rolling Stones*, *No Stone Unturned*, or *Stone Age* and cheap-looking covers. From a fan point of view, while some of those Klein releases had no added value for the owner of the previously released albums, except for the new cover with great unreleased photos, some releases did contain previously unreleased or difficult-to-find material including singles, B-sides, and outtakes. From then on, compilation and greatest hits albums would contain songs from either the early years or the post-1970 period, but not both. It would take until *Forty Licks*, released in 2002, for both sides to agree on a career-spanning compilation album, followed by *Grrr!* in 2012.

By May 1969 the Stones had another problem to deal with: Brian. He had been a problem for some time. Now it could no longer be postponed. With now two drug busts on his record (the second in 1968), he had no hope of getting the work permit for a major American tour. For two or three years, Brian had been slowly isolating himself from the other band members, musically, person-ally, and health-wise. Being psychotically paranoid, Brian saw self-fulfilling conspiracies everywhere. Mick and Keith, the songwriting team, had deprived him of the band's leadership and blocked him from composing songs, and the shift from psychedelic pop back to basic rock deprived him of the pleasure of being a "colorist" on exotic instruments. Playing just the guitar literally bored him to death. His asthma-worn lungs suffered above average from his ever-increasing drug use, and Anita Pallenberg's switch to his bandmate Keith did not help either. During the recording sessions for *Beggars Banquet*, he would lie on the studio floor or sit in the corner weeping and was largely useless, if present at all. The others agreed that he should not be allowed to block the band's future. "Though Brian must be sacked if the Stones were to survive, Jagger now agreed it must be on terms as tactful and generous as possible."[67] The offer was that Brian be asked to leave to allow the Stones to tour America, that for fans and press it would be a temporary absence allowing him to work on solo projects, and that he would keep his royalty share from past albums and a lump sum of £100,000 as acknowledgment for his musicianship and contribution to the band.

The Stones hired John Mayall band guitar virtuoso Mick Taylor, seven years their junior with angelic hair and face. Mick had called Mayall to propose a successor to Brian; Mayall proposed Mick T. The deal offered was not full equity membership. Mick T. would join the Stones as an employee for a salary of £150 per week. If things proved satisfactory, he would get a share of concert fees and record royalties.[68] On June 9 the press announced that Brian had resigned from the Stones because of disagreements over musical policy.

The initial plan to induct Mick T. slowly into the Stones was affected by Eric Clapton's invitation to join his new supergroup Blind Faith in the first-ever free concert in Hyde Park on July 5, 1969. In the night from July 2 to 3, the Stones were rehearsing with Mick T. and recording Steve Wonder's passionate "I Don't Know Why (I love You So)" (released on *Metamorphosis*), when news reached them that Brian had drowned in his swimming pool. Two days later at the Hyde Park concert, Mick, dressed-up like a reincarnation of Oscar Wilde, recited a poem by Percy B. Shelley (*Adonais*), released several ten thousands of half-dead butterflies, and inaugurated the post-Brian era with a powerful performance of "Jumping Jack Flash."

Brian's death remains a mystery until today. What looked like an accident—drowning in a swimming pool while stoned—may have been involuntary manslaughter. One theory suggests that a dispute arose between Brian and a construction worker, which escalated when Brian behaved condescendingly. There are many instances where Brian was snobbish, condescending, and furiously irritating. It was a sad ending for the founding father of the world's greatest band. Rumors allege that Mick and Keith cynically boycotted Brian's funeral while Charlie and Bill attended, but a recent documentary explains

---

67 Norman, *Stones*, 309.
68 Ibid., 318.

that Brian's family had made clear that Mick and Keith were not welcome at the event.

Brian's death turned out to simplify things for the band. There had been a concern about how to communicate the departure of the much-admired Brian in a way that did not antagonize the fan base, hence the agreed narrative about the temporary leave. Now they not only had a communication issue, but on top of this they had a martyr. The Hyde Park concert was certainly not a farce, but in their usual professionalism the Stones knew well how to combine genuine sorrow with band strategy. Moreover, they could present angel-faced Mick Taylor as Brian's legitimate heir, not as his replacement. And with Mick T. the Stones struck a fantastic bargain. For only an admittedly decent salary they now had one of the best guitarists on the payroll, which was less costly than paying Brian's full share. And, last but not least, Mick T. made a fantastic contribution to the band. Charlie remembers in a more recent interview how much Mick T. enhanced the artistic credibility of the Stones at a time where guitar virtuosi determined the status of a band. Mick T. was only slightly below Jimi Hendrix, Jimmy Page, or Eric Clapton, and his play was stunningly beautiful.

However, this upside quickly led to a downside as it changed the interpersonal dynamics and affected the roles held by other band members. The recruitment of Mick and his use as classic "lead guitarist" was a departure from the two-guitar doctrine that the band had adopted at its inception. Keith was now forced to play "rhythm," and he developed an inferiority complex that may have contributed to his severe drug addiction that would peak in 1973. Paradoxically, it was during that period that Keith developed some of his greatest power riffs in songs such as "If You Can't Rock Me," "Dance Little Sister," or "Hand of Fate." Ironically, just as Brian was impacted by the emerging Mick–Keith tandem, Keith was becoming affected by the two Micks. When Mick T., a few years later, no longer able to sustain the rock 'n' roll touring lifestyle which peaked in those years and allegedly frustrated over the band's crediting policy (like Bill), decided to leave the band, his resignation was met with some cynicism about his angelic face, cocaine addiction, and the simple fact of leaving. "Mick the quitter" became a label that stuck with him for many years. Soon replaced by the clownesque Ronnie Wood, a master in the art of dissimulating his fantastic musicianship under a continuous grin, Keith found a cool ally and drinking buddy who helped him gain back his self-esteem.

The Stones were, once more, low on cash. The only way to quickly earn some money was to plan their long-postponed next US tour, the first tour since 1967, independently from Klein who at that time had set sail for the Beatles' Apple company. To avoid an open rift, they asked Klein's nephew Ronnie Schneider to handle it. Artistically, touring had become a challenge. In the 1967 pop age, all that was required was to make an audience scream. By 1969, pop had evolved into rock, culture, and consciousness.[69] "Rock was not only a thousand watts louder; it was also a thousand times more serious."[70] A challenge the Beatles would avoid. The Stones sought help from the more experienced The Who, who seconded their Peter Rudge to assist. Peter's mission was to put together a self-sustaining touring crew, with its own maintenance, security, and publicity staff, and their own compere, Sam Cutler. They would take over the traditional prerogative of local promoters and hire their own supporting acts, B. B. King and Ika & Tine Turner. Mick had to find a new hatch, since long-haired singers had become legion. He found it in Tina. Mick "would stand each night and watch her, his body absorbing her mannerisms like data being fed into a computer."[71] On the way to the first show in Colorado, Mick suddenly realized they had nobody to introduce the band. He asked Sam Cutler to do it. Sam did not think about the words until he went on stage and then spontaneously uttered into the microphone the words that crossed his mind: "The Greatest Rock 'n' Roll band in the World, the Rolling Stones." Mick was furious. "Don't say that about us."[72] Somehow, there must have been a subsequent change of mind, as Sam's words are still audible today at the beginning of *Get Yer Ya-Ya's Out!*, the legendary live album covering the tour. What was it that Mick did not like: the "greatest in the world" or the "Rock 'n' Roll band"? Maybe Mick disliked being confined to a particular and narrowly defined musical style just after the flop of the Rock 'n' Roll Circus TV show, and rightly so. In the 1963–1969 period the Stones recorded few typical rock 'n' roll songs, mostly Chuck Berry covers, but literally only a handful out of a repertoire of around 80 to 100 songs, of which many were quite poppy and soulish. Mick may have thought—before changing his mind—that this label which referred to a rather homogenous musical style might undermine the strategy to position the Stones as a more artsy and "hip" phenomenon appealing to the cultural avant-gardes. It may also reflect a new self-awareness that the Stones had the potential to become a lasting operator on the market

---

69 Ibid., 349.

70 Ibid.

71 Norman, *Stones*, 354.

72 Pete Fornatale, *50 Licks—Myths and Stories from Half Century* (Bloomsbury, 2013), 110.

for socially relevant rock music, not just a short-term hit machine to disappear after two years. Having just changed country, management, and fiscal strategy, it was clear that the Stones had a future; they had to control it to the greatest possible extent, all the more as it was uncertain. From this perspective, the uncontrolled verbal outburst of Sam Cutler posed a problem. In hindsight, not erasing the words from the album was probably a smart move. By 1969 it was already clear that the Stones were not just a rock 'n' roll band like, for example, Status Quo but had a much more sophisticated societally relevant artistic proposition. But what is cooler, in combination with a "hide-and-seek" communications style, than to pretend being a common man while secretly aspiring at ennoblement? Alternatively, there may have been an element of self-derision, a verbal "tongue-in-cheek." What began with a hesitation evolved to a constitutionally enshrined doctrine: a few years later the Stones titled one of their hottest albums *It's Only Rock 'n' Roll (But I Like It)*.

The two sold-out shows grossed $260,000, breaking the Beatles' record, and quintupling the Beatles' share of the box-office receipts. It was a fantastic start. Some media, however, would criticize the Stones' exorbitant ticket prices ranging from $4.50 to $7.50: marginally higher than prices for the Doors or Blind Faith. "Paying six and seven dollars for an hour of Stones … says a very bad thing to me about the artists' attitude to the public. It says they despise their audience" (Ralph J. Gleason).[73] The Stones themselves were outraged by the $8.50 top price charged by local managers at LA Forum.

Having missed Monterey due to their drug problems back in the UK, and not being invited to Woodstock, the Stones thought about organizing their own festival, at least a free concert for some hundred thousand fans. The problem of finding an open space of sufficient size was solved when Craig Murray, president of the Sears Point Raceway, offered land at no charge and on minimal conditions, notably that any profits should benefit Vietnamese orphans. When the stage was almost built, and thousands of fans started to arrive, a fatal flaw revealed itself. The land Murray had generously proposed was owned by Filmways, an LA-based movie company, which asked for movie rights or one million dollars in cash. Mick hired San Francisco top litigator Melvin Belli, known for defending Charles Manson and Jack Ruby, Lee Harvey Oswald's killer, to sort out the mess. One day before the concert, Belli found an alternative venue: the Altamont Raceway near Livermore, California. Within hours the stage had to be dismantled, moved, and rebuilt, but most logistics

---

73 Norman, *Stones*, 357.

issues (e.g., toilets) were not appropriately solved. Someone had hired the Hells Angels for security. On Saturday, December 6, the concert started in a charged atmosphere of drug abuse and violence. When Jefferson Airplane performed "Revolution," the Angels would close in around a black youth. Airplane singer Marty Balin tried to intervene but was bludgeoned unconscious. While Gram Parson's Flying Burrito Brothers and Crosby, Stills, Nash & Young played their sweet anodyne country rock, further chaos broke out, with Angels beating up spectators at random. The Stones delayed their stage entry, with rumor having it that Mick wanted total darkness so that the stage lights would create best effects. By the time the Stones entered the stage, the Angels had already taken control of it. When Mick entered the site, a youth punched him in the face, crying, "I hate you, you fucker. I want to kill you."[74] Recordings reveal the anxiety in Mick's voice. "Will you give me some room? Will you move back, fellers, please?"[75] The Stones played their songs half tempo and in minor to calm the crowd, but in vain. "Now came the moment when ... Mick Jagger's intuition deserted him or his vanity became overmastering. Either way, the result was incredible stupidity. Folding his cloak around him, he stepped forward in the mincing gait he had evolved for this most presumptuous of all his masquerades,"[76] the Devil. Mick started "Sympathy for the Devil." "The effect was as sudden as if the ground had opened up."[77] He could not finish the song, so much was the violence during which young Meredith Hunter was stabbed to death by the Angels. The Stones were in shock, and all partying was canceled. Rolling Stone's conclusion was unequivocal: no one else but the Rolling Stones bore the primary responsibility for what had happened (maybe the Stones had better acquired that stake).[78] On December 5, one day before the darkest day in Stones history, their latest album had been released, *Let It Bleed*. A speculative question is whether the Stones would have modified the album title had the album not yet been released on Altamont day.

As terrible as these events were, one might disagree with the insinuation that the Stones, or Mick, lightheartedly risked human lives for better light effects, although Mick's admiration for the work of Leni Riefenstahl is no secret. The audio recordings of the event clearly suggest that the situation was

---

74 Ibid., 370.
75 Ibid., 373.
76 Ibid.
77 Ibid.
78 Ibid., 379.

out of control long before Mick went on stage and that he was genuinely scared and repeatedly attempted to calm the crowd. Breaking off the concert would have provoked chaos. Also, it was not visible for those on stage what exactly happened in the turbulent audience. There may have been negligence but not recklessness. Also, Mick may be vain but not crazy. His wildness is just for (the) show and unlike Jim Morrison he never confused stage persona and reality. According to photographer Jean-Marie Périer, who toured with the Stones between 1965 and 1973, Mick is the most normal person as soon as he gets off the stage, "a gentleman who gets up when a woman enters the room." A son of a Catholic sports teacher who taught his sons physical discipline, Mick is a control freak who exercises daily, eats healthy, drinks little, and ventures into light drugs only occasionally. Throughout his life, Mick applied to himself what he once said about Tom Waits: "You should only let yourself go if you can bring yourself back." The Altamont event may have been the only moment where he failed.

2. Laying Foundations

In autumn 1968, Christopher Gibbs introduced Mick to Prince Rupert Loewenstein of the merchant bank Leopold Joseph. Mick had realized they had made a mistake in teaming up with Allen Klein. Mick knew the group was doing well, yet they did not see any money. Mick asked Gibbs for help. Gibbs would try Deloitte, Price Waterhouse, and several law firms, but no one had the know-how to help them out. Prince Rupert did. He agreed to look at the papers and quickly became Mick's financial adviser. "Essentially the band were handcuffed on the one side by their contract with Allen Klein and on the other to Decca records, and my job was going to be to allow them to escape, Houdini-like, from both with minimum damage."[79]

Mick Jagger and Prince Rupert, the arch-Catholic aristocrat who despised rock music, what a team!—a seemingly surprising connection unless one remembers the Catholic roots of the Jaggers. Prince Rupert was literally the financial savior of the Stones, and after rescuing them from bankruptcy and fiscal turmoil, he laid the ground for their financial wealth. He will be omnipresent in the story from here on, at least behind the scenes. Interestingly, both the Beatles and the Stones teamed up with a very senior person (senior in

---

79 Prince Rupert Loewenstein, *A Prince Among Stones, That Business with The Rolling Stones and Other Adventures* (Bloomsbury, 2013), 86.

both age and professional capacity). The Beatles had George Martin—their musical director to whom the world owes many beautiful piano and string arrangements that frequently accompany Beatles songs. The senior person of the Stones is Prince Rupert—not a musician but a financial expert. The Stones owe him their wealth; the fans owe him the perennity of the Stones as a group. His financial and fiscal planning, constantly adapted, adjusted, and improved over the years, gave the band the funds necessary to spend as much time in the studio as it took to make the band members, in particular, Keith, satisfied with the results. Most bands have a limited budget and can only afford limited studio time. The recording must be completed within that time frame, and it inevitably ends up being conventional. Single artists have the additional burden of having to use hired musicians with no group-feel connection whatsoever. Not so the Stones. Keith ("I am more a record maker than a guitarist") could spend months in the studio, and up to ten days and nights without sleep, wrecking nerves and health of the studio personnel. Like a painter, he would add an additional lick here and there, using different guitars to achieve desired sound effects, then meshing everything together to come up with the right blend, which remains mysterious even to the most dedicated listener. That is why fans listen to Stones' albums over and over again without ever getting bored. It was the financial genius of Prince Rupert which made this artistic achievement possible. Money was not the only driver; according to Keith, going on stage is good for "ego gratification." However, the money was the financial basis for the colorful rest.

Around that time in 1968, Mick's friend Jann Wenner started *Rolling Stone* magazine. He invited the Stones to pick up 49 percent of the shares. Mick could not raise the money required, that is, the amount of £5,000. Mick turned to Prince Rupert who urged his partners to agree to the advance. However, the approval came too late, and the opportunity was missed.[80] It is hardly believable that the world-famous Stones could not raise £5,000 in cash while living in mansions and driving Rolls-Royces. The Stones could have had a controlling shareholding in an almost eponymous magazine that would soon become legendary. But cash was short, despite the band doing well. Prince Rupert's merchant bank was not yet ready to invest in the rock business, and that is why he eventually left it. This being said it may have been a blessing in disguise. It would be rather awkward if the Rolling Stones controlled a magazine with almost the same name, covering rock music including the Stones. Conflicts

---

80 Ibid., 75.

of interest would have been inevitable. Could the Stones have influenced the magazine's editorial policy? Would they have resorted to "self-preferencing," that is, orchestrating praise for themselves while criticizing others? Clearly, the articles and interviews published by an independent Rolling Stone did more for Stones myths than a controlled paper could have done. Finally, it avoided potential antitrust risks. The Stones being a dominant gatekeeper, less successful bands could complain to antitrust authorities about the magazine being less than neutral, alleging potential foreclosure effects.

Shortly after, Prince Rupert advised the Stones to free themselves from Decca and Klein. "Drop Klein and out. You've got to do that."[81] Brian's death complicated this task, as all the contracts were signed by Brian. Prince Rupert sought help from law firm Theodor Goddard and analyzed truckloads of contracts, a task that took 18 months, right until 1970 when these contracts expired and were open for renegotiation. Help from US lawyers was needed to find a way out of this situation; they were generally much more aware of the realities of the music industry than their UK counterparts.[82] Prince Rupert would hire Harold Orenstein, Peter Parcher, and Lloyd Cutler. Allen Klein hired Max Freund, and Decca hired Rowe & Moore. On July 30, spokesman Les Perrin's office confirmed that the Stones had terminated their relationship with Klein and Decca. Shortly afterward, the Stones filed suit in the New York State Supreme Court seeking $29 million in damages from Klein claiming that he had used their money to personal ends. "The legal battle would be long" (Loewenstein).

Decca made efforts to renegotiate the contract with the Stones. The documents Prince Rupert inspected showed that Decca had copyrights for all the work the Stones had done or "had started but not finished." This included any demos or half-finished scraps. Stones friend Marshall Chess from Chess Records happily represented to Decca's Eric Easton that they had the full list of songs. However, he later told the Stones' lawyers, hooting with laughter,

---

81 Ibid., 99.
82 "This brings one to an important distinction between American and British lawyers. British lawyers at the time certainly would never have tried to be managers and involve themselves in taking a role which they were not trained for or not able to do, whereas in America lawyers, like the Eastmans, were already taking on those responsibilities." Ibid., 93.

that "there's a huge amount of songs we've not talked about!"[83] This had to be disclosed to Decca, making litigation even harder.

Debts had to be repaid, and money had to be found to pay the 83 percent to 98 percent taxes the Stones owed and for which no provision had been made.[84] Bill Wyman received a tax claim for £118,000. He was shocked and realistic: "Once you owe £118,000 you never catch up."[85] Bill was not the only Stone concerned. Prince Rupert had to deliver worse news. The UK Inland Revenue Service audited the Stones thoroughly, finding it hard to believe that all these contracts led to no payment. The case went to court. Prince Rupert advised the Stones that they had to abandon their UK residence to avoid high British taxes. Prince Rupert looked around to find a suitable country. Ireland, Holland, Sweden, Denmark, and Germany were not safe taxwise, and America seemed undoable. Thus, he settled on France. The city of Paris hinting at 7/7 police surveillance for drug convicts, Prince Rupert asked Maître Jean Michard-Pellissier to negotiate the tax position with the *préfet* for the Department Alpes-Maritimes in the South of France. A deal was struck whereby the Stones could reside and would only pay a negotiated income tax. Settling tax issues was even more important as exchange controls existed at that time (these arrangements would later blow up because of Keith's drug problems). Prince Rupert then drew up a shortlist of suitable properties to purchase freehold, for tax reasons. Charlie and Bill did; Mick and Keith chose not to acquire property. Keith rented the famous Nellcôte property. After a short UK Goodbye–tour in March 1971 covering London, Birmingham, Manchester, Bristol, Leeds, Newcastle upon Tyne, Glasgow, Brighton, Coventry, and Liverpool, the tax exile began on April 5, 1971.

Two days later, on April 7, the Stones signed a new recording contract with Kinney Services, the US parent of Ahmet Ertegun's Atlantic Records. The contract covered six albums to be delivered over four years. They would be released on the Stones' own new label, Rolling Stones Records, but manufactured and distributed by Atlantic in the United States until 1984, by WEA Records in the United Kingdom until 1977, and in the 1978–1983 period by EMI. In the 1986–1991 period the Stones' music was distributed in the United States by Columbia and outside the United States by CBS. Rolling Stones

---

83 Ibid., 97.
84 Ibid., 90.
85 Norman, *Stones*, 391.

Records would only be dissolved in 1992 when the band signed a distribution deal with Virgin Records.

Head of the new label was Marshall Chess, the son of Leonard, the founder of the Chicago-based Chess label, whose records Mick would mail-order during his teenage years. The label's logo, the red-lipped tongue, would become one of the world's best known and most identifiable logos in commercial history. It had been designed by John Pasche, at that time a student in his final year of a graduate design course at the Royal College of Art in London. He worked on the logo for a week, was paid fifty pounds, and got an additional £200 in 1972 in recognition of the logo's success. A few days later, the first Rolling Stones album was released on the new label, *Sticky Fingers*, with its famous Andy Warhol–designed sleeve cover.[86] The Rolling Stones Records and its associated labels are owned by the Dutch company Musidor B.V., established in Herengracht 566 in Amsterdam (the Netherlands), which in turn is owned by the Rolling Stones, through Promotone B.V.

Subcontracting and outsourcing noncore tasks to specialists, whether musicians or designers, are sign of good business acumen and contribute to a company's efficiency. But there are probably few service providers who have added that much value to their principal's brand for so little reward. And it must have been difficult for young John to turn the page. Wherever he went, in every commercial mall, tourist shop, and street, he would face the omnipresent tongue on T-shirts, badges, and the like. However, the Stones do not forget good deeds. We shall see that they involved Pasche when redesigning the tongue in the early 2000, and more recently they involved him in their merchandising efforts around the Carnaby shop in London.

In her memoirs, Marianne Faithfull, who had a legitimate claim to authorship for "Sister Morphine," a song that eventually ended up on *Sticky Fingers*, describes how she rushed into a record store to purchase a copy of *Sticky Fingers*, as if she was suspecting that the boys had—like in so many other cases— appropriated the credits to themselves. When she pulled the album out of the sleeve, her concerns proved right, at first sight. The credits stated the usual "Jagger/Richards." Understandably she was appalled by that unacceptable level of blatant egoism and wrote a furious letter to the Stones' company. As it turns out, the answer was quite surprising: Mick and Keith had already sent a letter to their publishing company in respect of Marianne's credits. They initially wanted to give her the credits on the album but found out that if they

---

86 Ibid., 395.

had done so, Marianne's record company would have cashed in all the royalties, leaving nothing for her. To avoid that result, Mick and Keith had given instruction to pay one-third of the song royalties to her. One-third is maybe not as generous as it could have been, but it was at least something. Likely the song had a greater career under the Stones flag than it might have had under Marianne's own name, thus resulting in a better overall financial outcome for Marianne. As Germany's creative and charismatic antitrust attorney Jörg Karenfort says about crediting, "30% can be more than 100%." And considering the Stones' habit of endless studio work, it was probably justified that they took their own share of credits. And last but not least, they were Jagger/Richards. In his recent autobiographic documentary, Ronnie answers a question about financial inequality among the Stones with a deep sigh: "Well, that's also part of rock 'n' roll." The outcome may not have been optimal for Marianne, but it was not unfair. On Keno's Gasland, a fan reported a few years ago that both Marianne and Anita were still on the payroll of the Stones' company, and Marianne may still be today. They were not "thrown away" when their romantic relationships with Mick and Keith ended, maybe also to ensure their positive attitude toward curious media. Marianne's story mirrors a human tendency to react impulsively to perceptions driven by susceptibility. How often do people react negatively to an email received from a colleague based on suppositions that may be far from the reality and the intention behind the message sent.

3. Exploring the Boundaries

Tax exile life was not that easy in those days; there were many strains. Charley's wife Shirley was involved in an altercation with a customs officer at Nice airport and sentenced to six months' imprisonment. The Appeal Court in Aix-en-Provence reduced the sentence and suspended what was left of it. With Decca launching an avalanche of substandard albums using half-finished tracks recorded during their expired contract, the Stones wanted to have a blockbuster album to support their 1972 US tour. Keith had the famous *Rolling Stones Mobile Unit* (the "Mighty Mobile") drive down to Nellcôte. It was a truck with a mobile state-of-the-art recording studio that gave the Stones mobility for the recording of their concerts and albums.[87] It allowed them to record in

---

87 The Mobile Unit was also rented out to other artists, and many classic rock albums have been recorded with its help (e.g., Deep Purple's *Machine Head*).

Keith's villa after Ian Stewart had carpeted the walls of the basement to reduce the echo. The Stones also rented it out to other acts such as Deep Purple for *Machine Head* and Frank Zappa. The Mighty Mobile was a precursor of modern communications technologies in that it blurred the boundaries between home and the office. The upside is that the Stones did not have to rent a recording studio. The average musician has a limited budget and cannot afford to rent a studio for more than a week. The Mighty Mobile allowed the Stones to do what they like best: take, retake, and polish songs until they are satisfied—or, to be more precise, until Keith is satisfied—which can take a very long time. The downside is with a home studio allowing endless recording, recording becomes endless, which eventually becomes a burden on those who are not center stage.

Indeed, since the *Sticky Fingers* sessions, recording became an ever-longer process, with the band members and production personnel living by Keith's erratic working schedule, which would further depend on the unpredictable hours of Keith showing up in the studio. "He worked on his own emotional rhythm pattern; if Keith thought it was necessary to spend three hours working on a riff, he'd do it while everyone else picked their nose"(Andy Johns).[88] Bill remembers them working every night from eight until three in the morning, but "not everyone turned up every night. This was, for me, one of the major frustrations of this whole period."[89] Although Keith had always been the loudest in blaming Brian for sleeping in the studio, Keith now lived "in a time zone all his own."[90] Two weeks of endless jamming did not produce a single usable track. "There's no doubt they are an incredible group, but I didn't understand why they had to sit and play the same number over and over again for nine hours or two days in order to get it right. It was Keith Richards more than anybody else, the way he formulated for getting the feel he wanted. He didn't communicate tremendously with the others. I mean, they just went along with it" (Glyn Johns).[91] Years later, Charlie Watts would summarize his first 25 years with the Stones in one sentence: "It was five years of playing and twenty years of waiting."

The tendency to take other people's time for granted is not limited to musical geniuses but can also be found in other types of professional services firms.

---

88 Bockris, *Keith*, 149.

89 Robert Greenfield, *Exile on Main Street: A Season in Hell with the Rolling Stones* (Da Capo, 2008), 99.

90 Ibid., 100.

91 Bockris, *Keith*, 189.

Arguably, Keith was not a "diva" in the sense in which the word is used today, and at least he clearly is a musical genius and the waiting paid off, financially and artistically. Also, much emphasis is placed today on proper communication within the team. There is of course a structural reason for why there was little communication back then. The artistic genius typically is a perfectionist, and most artists—including painters, writers, poets and composers—work alone. But this is not true in the case of comic book authors, who commonly split the drawing task from the storytelling. Movie directors and actors don't work alone either. Even where they work in teams like, for example, members of symphony orchestras, they do not have to be in the same room at the same time. Even conventional rock music recording takes place mostly in tranches, with instrumentalists coming to the studio separately to record their part. But where the recording process is based on jamming, as it was in Nellcôte, things are inevitably different.

In August 1971, independent *Rolling Stone* magazine published an epic interview with Keith conducted by Robert Greenfield during his stay of 10 days at Nellcôte. It was a big step in establishing Keith's 1970s image.

While Mick T. had given the Stones' sound a new dimension, his playing "lead" destroyed the whole concept of the two-guitar band. Being the youngest member of the band and quite solitary, Mick T. would quickly become the scapegoat. "I could not believe how rude they were. To each other, really" (Rose Taylor).—"I remember Keith really humiliating him in front of people a couple of times. ... 'You play too fucking loud.' ... 'You're great live but in the studio you just don't make it'" (Andy Johns).[92] Several members of the entourage developed severe drug habits during the interminable nightly recording sessions. One day, during a warm-up session with Bobby Keys on sax and Jimmy Miller on drums, Keith suddenly came up with "Happy," which would become his lifelong signature song.[93]

As a result of drug busts in October 1971 and charges being filed, the Stones had to leave France in a hurry. Mick and Keith moved to LA where they started overdubbing and mixing the basic tracks recorded in France. This turned out to be an endless and hence utterly expensive process. Two or three weeks were spent on recording and mixing "Tumbling Dice" alone; there were fifteen to twenty-five hours of recorded material on just that song.[94] Marshall

---

92 Greenfield, *Exile on Main Street*, 129.

93 Ibid., 141.

94 Ibid., 171.

Chess remembered: "At the beginning, I'm not saying it never entered my mind that they had no idea what they were doing. ... But overall ... it would eventually come together. They would just lock. That was what they had. They had this magical ability, the alchemy of elements, that combined into one. ... They wouldn't see each other sometimes for seven months and within two days they would be playing like they were one person, locked together."[95] Dr. John worked a full week on "Let It Loose," and Bill had many of his bass parts overdubbed by jazz pioneer Bill Plummer's rollicking upright bass, which helped turn the album into a success. "There was a lot of lubricating going on. ... But they also knew exactly what they wanted. I did four tracks in about two hours, shook everybody's hand, went home" (Plummer).[96] Plummer earned the standard fee of a few hundred dollars but earned eternal fame among fans reading the album liner notes. While views diverge as to whether the Stones had a plan when starting recording, there is unanimity that this collective process was necessary to bring about the fantastic end result. For many later albums, the Stones would practice remote working long before COVID-19, with band members emailing their bits to the others. However, before each tour the Stones would set up a couple of weeks for live rehearsals in a tax-friendly location.

From LA, Keith would be flown to Vevey, Switzerland, to undergo a drug detox treatment. The Stones' solicitor Paddy Grafton-Green flew to Switzerland, sat at Keith's bed, and advised Keith that it would be a good time to make his will.[97]

Exile on Main St. was finally released on May 12, 1972,[98] the only rock album "to contain a reference to tax planning in its title."[99] On the very same day it was announced that the Stones' $29 million lawsuit against Klein had been settled out of court with the help of Prince Rupert, Ahmet Ertegun, and Mickey Rubin, Frank Sinatra's lawyer. Klein probably owed the Stones up to $17 million, but the Stones' NY lawyers advised to accept a $2 million settlement to get quick cash. Of these, $1 million was for Mick and Keith for songwriting and publishing; the rest was split five ways between the four Stones and Brian's estate—so much for partnership spirit. Mick and Keith agreed to pay Bill and

---

95 Ibid., 175.
96 Sandford, *Fifty Years*, 241.
97 Greenfield, *Exile on Main Street*, 185.
98 Norman, *Stones*, 403.
99 Loewenstein, *A Prince Among Stones*, 102.

Charlie another $50,000 each out of their pockets to make them accept the proposal.[100] The Stones had to continue recording and touring to finance their expensive lifestyle to which they had become accustomed. "The Stones were now free to record for a company of their choice and the sum they obtained would be greater than their old contractual commissions which had been withheld pending negotiations. They did not preclude us from future litigation since Klein found point after point of increasing triviality which had to be put before the New York courts and the federal courts. In the case against them and the [UK] Inland Revenue there were lawsuits spread over seventeen years."[101]

Exile sold some 800,000 copies following the release. Each copy was sold at 50 cents (2 × 25 cents because it was a double album), that is, it grossed $400,000. Its production cost had reached the astronomical level of $500,000. As composers, Mick and Keith would get a mechanical royalty of two pennies per track, and because they published the music themselves, it was all for them. The other band members shared in the artists' royalties, usually 5 to 6 per cent of the list price minus a production allotment. In total, the Stones would get between 25 and 32 cents per album sold (out of 50 cents). The Stones would only make some profit because they had a better recording deal than most other acts.[102]

In 1972, the Stones had been together for 10 years. "In the rockbiz, this is unheard of. Completely. They were royalty. No, even better, they were kings. Undeniably. By acclamation. And it was to America they came to seize their crowns."[103] Their planned US tour was intended to be a thoroughly professional and respectable event, twice as long as the 1969 tour. Everything would be planned to the smallest detail. No more late concerts. For the first time, the Stones would meet to rehearse thoroughly, from 6:00 p.m. to 6 a.m. over a couple of nights before the start of the tour in a small movie house in Montreux. Canada was chosen for fiscal reasons. Mick also insisted on rehearsing in a building that resembled the large halls they would play in.[104] The Stones would boil down a set list that remained unchanged throughout the tour. The tickets were sold at $6.50, with a limit of 2 tickets per buyer. To mark the difference

---

100 Greenfield, *Exile on Main Street*, 195.
101 Loewenstein, *A Prince Among Stones*, 108.
102 Robert Greenfield, *Stones Touring Party, A Journey Through America With the Rolling Stones* (Dutton, 1974), 201.
103 Ibid., 17.
104 Ibid., 33.

from the 1969 tour, the Stones initially wanted small venues as a sign of contrition for their Altamont disaster. Economics, however, revealed that the tour had to gross $2 million to be profitable. There was thus no alternative to large cities, arenas, and audiences. Prince Rupert educated the Stones about cost management. He brought lawyers and accountants to every business meeting so that issues were discussed in the presence of the band. He also explained that putting the whole entourage in five-star hotels would make the tour very expensive and reduce profits. Prince Rupert reversed the classic model of a band "working the album", that is, touring to promote an album for the benefit of the record company, the latter paying a modest contribution to the tour expenses. Prince Rupert thought that the album should support the tour, and a tour should be a means of generating revenue for the band not the record company. Again, Peter Rudge handled the tour, building a logistics operation based on the principle that nothing must be left to chance. For the first time, the Stones traveled with their own stage. While the equipment would travel overland in a fleet of trucks, the Stones had a comfortably sized private jet. A range of subtly graded backstage passes was issued with Peter's countersignature; they bore the letters STP, Stones Touring Party. In Detroit, 120,000 applications had been received for 12,000 seats. In Chicago, 34,000 tickets sold out in 5 hours. In LA, the $6.50 concert ticket was sold for $75 on the black market.[105] "Ticket scalping," that is, the reselling of concert tickets at inflated prices, was a specialty of tour promoters. They would urge the band to keep the ticket prices low and resell large chunks of tickets for their own benefit. Record companies would also scalp tickets to give larger amounts of tickets to disc jockeys as a bribe. Bill Graham even printed different tickets for his friends and had them enter through a particular gate. "Scalping was endemic, all-pervasive. Touring, at that time, was essentially a deeply corrupt business." The tour accountants also had to make sure that there was no unaccountable cash in the tour. US tax fraud claims could easily put an end to a band's career. The Stones had succeeded in selling the tour to the media, and a range of photographers, journalists, and literary writers (e.g., Truman Capote) joined the tour to cover it. The Stones were taking a definite chance. Despite good ticket sales and media demand, they would do the same sort of show as in 1969, a classic set of 15 rock tracks and no encore. "What nobody could forecast was how the kids would react to it."[106]

---

105 Norman, *Stones*, 408.
106 Greenfield, *STP*, 46.

The tour was a total success. "It was a social event. It was a cultural event. It was a business event" (Greenfield).[107] It was the first modern rock 'n' roll tour. The Stones had reached Sinatra–Elvis status, were acclaimed by fans and media, and had earned some decent money.

By that time, the Stones were now contracted to another new Netherlands-based corporation called Promo-Tours, which was part of the Musidor group. New York–based Sunday Promotions, a firm created for the purpose of running the tour, signed a contract to pay Promo-Tours an agreed amount of money per tour, based on a guarantee or a percentage of the gross, whichever was higher. In most cases, the agreed percentage was 70 percent, that is, the promoter would keep 30 percent of the revenue, out of which he had to pay all expenses. On average the promoter would make around $5,000 profit per show, and a show would generate around $100,000. "You pay Sunday Promotions, you get the Stones, you keep the gross."[108] A top promoter like Bill Graham had a special deal whereby Sunday Promotions would pay his expenses and guarantee him an agreed profit. The tour grossed $3 million, with $1 million in expenses paid to the local promoters. The agreed payment to Promo-Tours was another expense. At the end of the tour, Sunday Promotions had earnings of $100,000. Of the $2 million paid to Promo-Tours, the latter withheld $600,000 for Dutch taxes. The rest of the money was used to pay the STP tour personnel, the additional musicians, and Peter Rudge's own company, Sound Images, all of which added up to $1 million. Each of the Stones is estimated to have earned $250,000, that is, $4,000 per day and $28,000 per week, more than twice what an average middle-class family would earn in a year. Still, the Stones were not the most profitable band. Acts like Leon Russell had fewer overhead costs, and Neil Young would work on a 90–10 split of the cake.[109]

4. Living in a Dangerous World

The Stones had now been together for a decade, and things had changed. Everyone had wives or firm partners, living their own lives. More importantly, the relationship between Mick and Keith had started to change during the Nellcôte period. Mick's newlywed wife Bianca did not want to mingle with the others and stayed in Paris, forcing Mick to absent himself regularly from Nellcôte. Anita and Keith rejected her violently.

---

107 Fornatale, *Myths*, 153.
108 Greenfield, *STP*, 199.
109 Ibid., 200.

A brief parenthesis: Adding a new person to a small bubble of people frequently leads to tension. Bianca Jagger was in some ways the Yoko Ono of the Rolling Stones. Both were perceived (except their partners) as "stiff upper class" and set to break the bonds between the boys. Bianca was even accused of ennobling her origins. Diversity and inclusion did not yet exist in rock 'n' roll. Women were considered posing a threat to the unity of bands of brothers. The artistic world confined women to the status of a muse, but their own talent was denied. Clara Schumann, Camille Claudel, or Alma Mahler could speak about this at length. To Bianca, even the status of a muse was denied. Her staying in Paris was criticized although Charlie himself once said that he "did not want to associate our wives with us on tour." Strange as it seems, race may have unconsciously played a role too, with Bianca being a Latin American and Yoko a Japanese. Western eyes may have looked at them with a degree of bias, imputing to them motivations of being interested. In hindsight, their biographies tell a different story. Yoko Ono was born into a conservative upper-class banker family at a time when Japanese girls were not supposed to pursue an eccentric artist career in New York. Her screaming is admittedly unsettling for Western ears. On "Well (Baby, Please don't Go")," where she and John are backed up by Frank Zappa and his Mothers of Invention, I initially took her for a saxophone. However, her more conventional songs are at least as good as the bulk of her late husband's later output, leaving a few highlights such as the song *Mind Games* aside. Bianca, in the many years since her divorce, had an impressive track record of charitable goodwill activity as ambassador of human rights causes, including for her country of origin. The fact that she never remarried (just like Mick) could be because she is authentically attached to the spiritual traditions of her upbringing. Both women deserve more recognition and respect in the fan communities of their respective bands. Parenthesis closed.

Mick would eventually take over the band leadership, assuming total control, giving the others "lectures" during business meetings (Stu).[110]

Atlantic Records demanded a new album. By the time Mick and Keith started to work on songs for the new album in Montreux, the creative spark between the two was ignited only by conflict.[111] This became the root problem of the new album. Mick and Keith were used to spending much time together

---

110 Sandford, *Fifty Years*, 253.

111 Bockris, *Keith*, 169. "Richard's partnership with Jagger, the longest-lasting close relationship of his life, was and is the only one that is essentially free of the addict's pattern of using others until they are used up, as Keith had done with Brian"(Ibid.).

to come up with songs; now Mick's marriage did not allow for that. Rather than strumming away together until they hit on something, Keith would thrust a song at Mick, and Mick would acknowledge receipt.

The Stones had to find a place for two to three months to record the new album called *Goats Head Soup*. Jamaica was one of the few locations where the Stones' various convictions for drug offenses did not matter legally. Japan, Canada, Australia, and the United States had barred the Stones from entry, and Britain was no option fiscally. In France charges were pending. Paul Simon recommended Dynamic Studios in Kingston. Keith discovered Jamaica as the "most musically conscious place," the only place to come up "with a really different kind of new music which still has the basic simplicity of rock 'n' roll" (Keith).[112] Keith would also feel the unique Jamaican approach to recording, where no one would prevent the musicians from experimenting technically with the recording equipment. Despite the optimal surroundings, the recording sessions were not living up to the usual standard. Mick had adopted a complacent attitude ("It's 1972. Fuck it. We've done it."); producers Jimmy Miller and Andy Johns had collapsed from drug abuse; and Keith was too weak to provide the creative impulses needed. *Melody Maker*'s Michael Watts remembered: "He looked very wasted, very frail. You expected this tough guy and he looked as if you could blow him over. ... Jagger was being very camp and louche but he was also very protective of Richards. I'll always remember that. Jagger came up and put his arms around him and talked to him and you knew that he was looking after his welfare. I think it became a terrific strain for Jagger to hold this guy up."[113] The drug use also deteriorated producer Jimmy Miller. "Jimmy Miller went in a lion and came out a lamb" (Keith). Jimmy was "sort of halfway in control of 'Sticky Fingers' but his grip was slipping a bit. On 'Exile' they sort of stopped listening to him and by the time we got to 'Goats Head Soup' it was like he wasn't there" (Andy Johns). "Jimmy was great, but the more successful he became the more he got like Brian. ... He ended up carving swastikas into the wooden console at Island Studios. It took him three months to carve a swastika. Meanwhile Mick and I finished 'Goats Head Soup.'"(Keith).[114] Jimmy was not invited to produce the next album of the Stones. *Goats Head Soup*, released in August 1973, was a commercial success but did not convince critics, despite some hit tracks ("Angie"

---

112 Ibid., 171.
113 Ibid., 173.
114 Fornatale, *Myths*, 165.

and "Heartbreaker") and some of the most mysteriously beautiful compositions ("Coming Down Again," "Winter," and "Can't You Hear the Music?").
The album "was so uncharacteristic in terms of what one had come to expect
of the Stones that it threw most people and alienated others"(Roy Carr).[115] In
hindsight, it takes a long time to recognize the particular genius of this album,
but over time it never stops growing on the listener. This is partially due to the
wobbly sound which appeals to the detective in the listening fan to figure out
what he actually hears.

Today there is much corporate talk about mental health, values, and being
supportive. If genuine and meant to be lived, it can be more than lip service.
The Stones' track record in this respect may seem ambiguous. When Brian was
fading away, Mick and Keith did not show a lot of support to him, although
Bill and Charlie were quite close to Brian. However, Brian may have refused
being helped, and he may have been a tragically helpless case given his drug
use and judicial record. Further, he stood in the way of Mick and Keith in the
power struggle for control of the band. Businesses are altruistic to a certain
level but not beyond. As French philosopher Paul Valéry wrote in his *Lettre à
l'esprit*, shortly after the end of World War I, men are inherently competitive.
Power struggles are everywhere, even in the local church choir. With Keith
ailing, things were different. Mick did care for Keith, and he did it in a remarkably affectionate way. That was certainly sincere. While Mick and Keith at
one point no longer needed Brian, Mick still needed Keith, and Keith needed
Mick.

After a very successful European tour in the summer of 1973, the Stones
would set up their tents in the Munich Hilton and the Musicland studios to
start recording "It's Only Rock 'n' Roll." Keith increasingly loved recording
just after finishing tours. Jimmy Miller being off the radar screen, Mick and
Keith would produce the album themselves under the name "The Glimmer
Twins." This time they did much better than with *Their Satanic Majesties
Requests*. Again, sessions would work through the nights. The Stones recorded
a total of four weeks in Munich and came out with a list of some 20 tracks, of
which 12–13 were shortlisted. Mick and Keith met in England in April 1974 to
finish recording the vocal parts. "We finished off writing the songs that hadn't
been completed lyric-wise, because a lot of them had been written in a very
loose framework to start with—maybe just a chorus, a hook line, or something.
Then we got on and did the vocals and I left Mick for a couple of weeks in to

---

115 Bockris, *Keith*, 176.

do his solo vocals because he often comes up with his best stuff alone in the studio with just an engineer. Then he doesn't feel like he's hanging anybody up" (Keith).[116] Creative people have their ideal working pattern, which cannot be changed without affecting the result. There is a possibility that Keith needs the presence of other people to be at his best, even if this means that others have to wait for hours, which is not disrespect, although it can be painful for the waiting others. Similarly, Mick may prefer solitude to do his work and not just out of disrespect for his fellow band members. A certain degree of flexibility as to individual working style preferences enhances the end result. For those in the waiting room the question is whether the overall result is worth the waiting. For Charlie it was but not for Bill (as we will see later).

While Mick worked on the vocal tracks, Keith hung out with Faces' guitarist Ron Wood in London to work on Ron's first solo album *I've Got My Own Album to Do.* When Mick called Keith to do some backup vocals on the Stones album, Keith replied that he had to finish work for Ronnie first. This is surprising as Keith was the band member always most insisting that the Stones should always be a priority. When Bill was the first Stone to release his colorful country rock solo album *Monkey Grip* in May 1974, Keith would call it "Monkey Shit." In reality, in Keith's work on Ronnie's album lay the seeds of their future solo careers.[117] In parallel, Ron had also called on Mick to contribute one song to his album ("I Can Feel the Fire").

Ron ended up as Keith's drinking buddy, but he was initially seen in a different role: that of a potential replacement. But not at all of Mick Taylor. To the contrary, Mick reportedly asked Ronnie whether he could replace Keith (just) on tour should Keith be unable to get a US visa. That would have been the Stones with Taylor and Wood on guitars—an interesting perspective that never materialized; it would have irreversibly destroyed the personal chemistry between Mick and Keith regardless of the artistic and operational merit. At that time, performing had become a necessity for Keith, as the required pre-tour cleanup was the only way to get him off heroin. His doctor advised at that time he had only six months to live if he did not stop taking drugs. Never before had Keith been so detached from the band. In the album's title song, written and recorded by Mick and Ronnie (with the Faces' Kenney Jones on drums), Keith was not involved at all. How strange to imagine that Keith had no part in what became one of the most frequently played stage rockers and

---

116 Ibid., 189.
117 Ibid., 190.

what more than anything else expressed the very essence of the Rolling Stones' credo.

It's Only Rock 'n' Roll was finally released in October 1974. Critics and long-term fans found it disappointing, but the album and its singles became enormous hits all over the world. *Creem* magazine voted it the best album of 1974, the Stones the best band, and their 1972 tour movie *Ladies and Gentlemen: The Rolling Stones* the best rock film.

It's Only Rock 'n' Roll represented the point at which Mick and Keith began to pull strongly in opposite directions.[118] When Keith proposed a summer tour, the band refused. Keith moved in with Ronnie for the whole summer, helped finish Ronnie's album, and performed live as a member of Woody and Friends.

In December 1974, the Stones were gearing up to record their next album, when Mick T. unexpectedly resigned from the band. Mick T. had repeatedly expressed frustration about not being credited for his contribution to songwriting. The resignation came as a shock, even more so as he finally seemed to have meshed perfectly into the group's overall sound. According to rock critic Robert Palmer, "Taylor was the most accomplished technician who ever served as a Stone. A blues guitarist with a jazzman's flair for melodic invention, Taylor was never a rock and roller and never a showman." The day after he quit, Keith sent him a telegram: "Really enjoyed playing with you for the last five years. Thanks for all the turn-ons. Best wishes and love." According to Mick T.'s wife Rose, "Mick just read it and started crying."[119] Frustration and humiliation may have been one reason for Mick T. He also wanted to do other types of music. Mick T. joined the Jack Bruce group, which broke up quickly due to feuds, and recorded some solo albums. It is, however, most surprising that a musician of Mick T.'s league did not manage to develop any sort of noticeable career after leaving the Stones. In more recent comments, Keith mentioned that Mick T. suffered from an almost inexplicable lack of self-confidence. When Mick T. reunited with the Stones on stage for a few dates throughout the 2010s, he did not seem very enthusiastic and looked as if he was still holding a grudge.

In January 1975, the Stones started their hunt for a replacement with auditions in Munich, where the Stones recorded music for their next album. Rumors have it that the auditions allowed the Stones to have great talent on their record without having to pay for it. The wish list included Jeff Beck, Mick

---

118 Ibid., 191.
119 Ibid., 194.

Ronson (Mott the Hoople), Peter Frampton, Ry Cooder, Rory Gallagher, and psychedelic virtuoso Harvey Mandel (formerly Canned Heat). The latter played the most remarkable guitar solo on *Black and Blue*'s opening number "Hot Stuff." Harvey was Mick's favorite candidate, but Keith preferred Wayne Perkins, a Texan of Cherokee descent.[120] Keith and Wayne spent a night drinking, and Wayne began to rehearse some 30–40 Stones songs for the next tour. Keith wanted to hire Wayne, Mick didn't. He wanted the new Stone to be an Englishman. Did fiscal considerations play a role? Ronnie, legally and morally committed to the Faces, had always declined, but the Faces were in the process of breaking up. On Sunday, March 30, Ronnie happened to be in Munich, inquiring with Keith about the progress of the search. Keith replied, "We're looking for a Brit who looks cool, with a fucking good sense of humour, who's slightly shorter than you, plays OK, likes a pint, won't freak out on the road, isn't going to jump ship and can get on with Jagger." Ron asked, "Where are you gonna find someone like that by next Friday?" Woody then played on a song called "Hey Negrita" (he is credited with "inspiring" the song, which means that he may have written the whole song, at least the music). Ron was immediately hired, initially just for the upcoming tour. "After literally one number, we thought: 'That's it. It's obvious'" (Keith).[121]

It quickly turned out that Ronnie was exactly what both Mick and Keith needed: a good-humored drinking buddy, go-between, mediator, and a—seemingly—not overly talented guitarist. He fit in perfectly. With him, the Stones reverted to their initial two-guitar style, and Keith no longer had to suffer from an inferiority complex. Stones' iconographers will notice that Ronnie brought a good dose of auto-derision and self-parody (back) to the band, and on photos the Stones would from then on smile more frequently than before. Some writers note that Ronnie also had the right look for the years to come, whose spirit was more virile and less effeminate. It may be better to say "less angelic," as Ronnie enjoys travesty quite a lot, as numerous official and social media pictures reveal. The eternal Benjamin of the band, Ronnie would stay with the Stones for 19 years as a salaried employee before finally making equity partner.

---

120 Wayne Perkins contributed to Bob Marley's worldwide fame. When Marley delivered the basic tracks for *Catch a Fire* to Island Records in London, the label's president Chris Blackwell considered the sound too unfamiliar for British and American audiences and asked Wayne Perkins to record the famous guitar riffs on "Stir It Up" and "Concrete Jungle." The rest is known.

121 Sandford, *Fifty Years*, 273.

One month later, on May 1, 1975, the Stones drove down Fifth Avenue on a flatbed truck announcing their US tour, the first after three years. Their new album was not yet released. For their 68-day and 27-city tour, each founding Stones earned $409K, $317K after tax, and about $10,000 before tax per show. Ronnie was paid $225,000, that is, $4,800 per concert before tax. It was more than what Ian McLagan was paid a few years later. But then, Ronnie was more than a keyboarder to the Stones. The Stones also sold more than a million copies of their (worthless) compilation *Made in the Shade*, which combined 10 tracks from the last four albums. Just as the later *Rewind*, the compilation is wholly uninspired, but the cover looks great. The enormously successful but also drug-fueled tour reinforced the cult status of the band. Annie Leibovitz toured with the band and made a fantastic photo book of the tour; some say that the drug-fueled tour experience turned out to be too much for her.

After the US tour, Mick moved to LA where he would hang out with John Lennon, and Keith moved back to Montreux. Bill released his second solo album *Stone Alone*. The Faces having broken up, Ron could join the Stones for good. The new album *Black and Blue* was finally released on April 16, 1976 (in the charts second only to ABBA), followed by a European tour. Just before going on stage of Les Abattoirs in Paris, Keith learned that his 76-day-old son Tara had suffered crib death. The show took place.

Several tracks of the Paris show made it on the double-live album *Love You Live* that would be released in 1977. The release was delayed for some time because Billy Preston asked for 12 percent of the gross revenue. In fact, during the 1975/1976 tour, Billy had a prominent place on scene. He was allowed to perform two or three songs per concert with his own group. The story is that he liked it so much that at one point he refused to leave the stage. Later he would unexpectedly claim a share in the royalties for the live album, which did not go down well with the Stones. Bill never again played with the Stones.

Keith was still in bad shape, just being able to play through the show. During the Munich concert, he nodded off after a guitar solo on "Memory Motel," in front of 20,000 screaming fans. Many reviews written on the 1975 and 1976 tours were extremely critical, including about Mick's singing style, announcing the expected end of a band that was only a parody of its former self. The Stones' sound had indeed changed a lot compared to the 1972 and 1973 tours. It was much rougher, the tempo less upbeat, and Mick's voice sounded more guttural and virile. Ron's blubber-guitar sound was the opposite of the Mick T.'s melodic play, and Ollie Brown's percussion would add to the funky touch of the music. Retrospectively, the tour combined old and new material in a fascinating manner. It was artistically audacious to reshape several classics, turning both the poppy "Get off of My Cloud" and the folksy "You Can't Always Get What You Want" into rough deconstructed blues numbers, which made *Love You Live* the most interesting of all Stones live albums.

During the winter following the tour, Keith relaxed with members of the Monty Python crew and recorded a raucous solo version of Chuck Berry's "Run Rudolph Run" with Toots and the Maytals. At the same time, Mick was in full control of the band and renegotiated the expiring US recording contract with Atlantic Records. Ahmet Ertegun offered the band $20 million for an extension. Mick agreed. It was the calm before just another storm that could have blown the Stones away.

On January 3, 1977, the US Drugs Enforcement Agency sent an information request to the British Home Office concerning Keith's latest trial. One week later, Keith appeared at Aylesbury crown court to face charges of coke and LSD possession. He pleaded not guilty. Mick flew in for support from his LA winter break with Linda Ronstadt. On January 12, Keith was convicted of coke possession. The judge decided against a jail term, but the next incident would inevitably lead to imprisonment. It was exactly 10 years since Keith's first stand in court. "An expensive habit," he commented.

Four days later, the Stones announced a £7 million distribution deal with EMI for all territories outside the United States. The four Stones flew to Toronto to prepare recording sessions in the El Mocambo club. When Keith followed on Thursday, February 24, Canadian Customs authorities welcomed him in force and arrested Anita. Dogs had sniffed a brick-sized chunk of hash in her handbag. Three days later Canadian Mountain Police (Keith first took them for EMI representatives in disguise) searched Keith's hotel room and discovered ample drugs and drug-related material. Keith was charged for drug trafficking; the charge carried a potential sentence from seven years to life. The press coverage that followed "was an even worse disaster than anyone had anticipated."[122] The *Toronto Star* speculated that Keith might go to jail and that "Mick Jagger and the rest were close to calling it quits."[123] The morning after Keith's arrest, Robert Stigwood's RSO label retracted its offer for a $7 million US recording deal. Prince Rupert called Mick to inform him that his bargaining power was significantly reduced. Three more record companies would withdraw from bidding for the Stones. While Keith appeared in court, the other Stones left Canada for New York: a breach of group etiquette

---

122 Ibid., 296.
123 Ibid.

for Keith. Again, Keith was lucky enough to escape, helped by an emergency medical visa issued by the US authorities. Keith retired to a farm for rehab in Pennsylvania first, then to a colonial home in South Salem, New York, where Mick in person would regularly bring him reggae tapes to listen to. "Mick looked after me with great sweetness, never complaining. He ran things. ... Mick looked after me like a brother" (Keith).[124] Tough and uncompromising on business issues, Mick can be a great and compassionate friend.

Times were unstable. Keith realized that in order to stay clean of heroin, he had to part from Anita. In the meantime, Ron had picked up some of Keith's bad habits and got busted himself. Bill threatened to quit the band. Charlie had grown to like raising sheepdogs at home. According to Charlie, Stu "thought the band he had helped found was badly off the rails."[125]

Whenever Keith was ailing, Mick genuinely and empathically looked after him, which did not prevent him from having a Plan B for the good of the band. Keith in turn collaborated well with Mick but there was also a lot of bitching and bickering involved, and it was two ways. None of this is truly surprising. Fate had connected two individuals from quite different social backgrounds, united by a shared passion. Their unexpected success condemned them to spend most of their lifetimes together. They were like a married couple except that they could not get a divorce. They were professionally and artistically interdependent. Each of them had his respective strengths and weaknesses, and as their later solo efforts would confirm, they only reached their full potential together. After Brian's demise, Mick and Keith had consolidated their co-leadership of the band. Now, with Keith coming down from drugs, Mick was compelled to assume band leadership alone. He had to take all the decisions himself. Once Keith resurrected, he naturally wanted to play his usual part again, which Mick in turn viewed as a power grab. What looks like an objectively justified evolution from the outside may be perceived as a hostile move from the inside. Collaboration between human beings has always been a question of interpretation and susceptibility, as is social life altogether. As the story of Cain and Abel tells us, jealousy is the second-oldest feeling after curiosity. Jealousy is driven by perception, a perception that is off objective reality. No one can easily escape jealousy. For the Stones as for any other business, the challenge is to overcome jealousy as otherwise there can be no long-lasting collaboration. If overcoming natural jealousy takes some ventilating, and if that ventilating

---

124 Ibid., 300.
125 Ibid., 301.

involves the verbalization of frustration, this in turn should not be perceived as an attack on authority. Rather, it helps to preserve the project. Another important factor is the ability to forgive. In *Leçons particulières*, Françoise Giroud observed the inclination of French politicians to repeatedly betray each other, and she was surprised by their willingness to forgive each other just as easily. In human relationships, offenses and betrayals, objective or perceived, are unavoidable. Hence the importance of being able to contextualize and to forgive. This is what the Bible has been teaching the world (or parts of it) for some three thousand years. The Stones, musically rooted in a biblical culture, seemed to have understood this, at least intuitively. The less biblical Beatles did not. The Beatles had much more creative talent than the Stones. However, the Stones were better at people management. They succeeded where the Beatles failed. It may have been a matter of anthropological alignment.[126]

5. New Faces

In the late 1970s, the Stones were in their mid-30s. The period of androgynous glam rock had come to an end, and the much more virile punk movement with bands such as the Sex Pistols in the UK or the New York–based Ramones were storming the charts. It was time for a relooking. When the Stones had signed the EMI deal, they obtained the free use of EMI's Pathé-Marconi studios in Paris, where Édith Piaf and Charles Aznavour had recorded. The Stones spent some six months in Paris recording *Some Girls*, to be engineered by new hire Chris Kimsey. The Stones decided to part from their plethora of usual auxiliaries such as Billy Preston or other sound colorists. Instead, Mick picked up the rhythm guitar. "They sound like bloody Status Quo" (Stu).[127] Later on, the Stones hired a young harmonica player called Sugar Blue (aka James Whiting) and former Faces keyboarder Ian McLagan. Both played on *Miss You*, which became the Stones' eighth number one hit in the United States and

---

126 This term intends to suggest that there is an implicit "order" built into the DNA of the universe, which must be factored in to ensure long-term viability of any social or economic conduct. For example, if I only eat French fries and neither vegetables nor fruit, I will bear the long-term consequences. If today I decide to stop breathing, I will feel the consequences much faster. The same principles apply to the social sphere, whether private or professional. If the Stones lasted for 60 years despite all their interpersonal tensions, they must have done something right: just as Philemon and Baucis, whom Greek mythology celebrates affectionately for their longtime relationship.
127 Sandford, *Fifty Years*, 302.

one of their greatest songs ever. After his contribution, broke and penniless Ian politely asked for his remuneration. Mick paid him out of his pocket the sum of 120 French francs (£15). The new album, rough and edgy, sold eight million copies; it toppled *Saturday Night Fever*. The album "resuscitated the Stones, just as 'Beggar's Banquet' had ten years earlier. … With Dylan no longer bringing it all back home, the Beatles mummified and Led Zep grounded, this was the Stones searching for—and finding—a new voice."[128]

Ian McLagan, the decade-long keyboarder of the Small Faces and the Faces and a musician of proven status, contributed to *Miss You* with his magnetic electric piano that is quite essential to the song's disco atmosphere. He must not have dared to ask for payment upfront, and it probably frightened him to ask the question even afterward. One imagines a slightly annoyed Mick searching his pockets for some bills and grudgingly handing them over (120 French francs were at that time the price for 20 merguez sandwiches). However, what looks harsh on a stand-alone basis translated into an extended collaboration, with Ian becoming a long-standing member of the touring family and occasionally contributing to a studio recording. He was also part of the New Barbarians venture. So, Ian's ad hoc generosity was probably more a sensible investment in a relatively lucrative long-term relationship.

With famous Ian McLagan making an essential contribution to one of the world's greatest hits for the price of a few sandwiches, one wonders whether Sugar Blue had to give it away for free. Stories that Mick picked him up while playing in the Paris metro station are probably legend. The more realistic version is that someone from the Stones entourage saw him play in a club or at a party, collected his phone number, and then gave it to Mick. Sugar Blue also does the incredible harp solo on "Down in the Hole" and another one on "Send It to Me." These two songs were recorded two years after *Miss You*. In the very hypothetical event that Sugar Blue was not paid for this first recording, he would certainly have been for the latter two.

With the new well-acclaimed album out, Keith wanted to tour. Mick was reluctant, telling the press he would not tour "with a geezer pushin' a heroin charge." However, Prince Rupert proposed a deal which would guarantee each Stone $800,000 for six weeks' work. As part of another Plan B, a discreet phone call was placed to Jimmy Page to check his availability just in case Keith would run into visa problems. The Stones met at Todd Rundgren's estate in Woodstock, New York, to rehearse for the tour, where Keith would

---

128 Ibid., 305.

again get hooked on heroin. "He was lying there. ... Mick and I would feed him. ... We'd cover him up with a blanket at night. It gave Mick a very good feeling to be able to help Keith" (Jerry Hall).[129] At the same time, Mick would run 10 miles daily through the New York woods to stay sober. Ian McLagan returned, and Mick negotiated a flat fee of less than $3,000 per concert, to avoid another Billy Preston–type holdup. The Stones' ninth US tour in summer 1978 was a modest success, but nevertheless a sign of changing times, with Mick abandoning the female diva attitude for a more pimp-like outfit (tight red-leatherette pants, white dinner jacket, and a rakishly tilted golf cap) and Keith and Woody parodying the punks' thrashing guitar style, all songs being played at double tempo. The stage outfit was minimalist and together with the set list, it reflected a back-to-basics approach. The tour was labeled the "Farewell Tour"; it was going to be their last. While it was not, this was the only tour in which Ronnie performed a significant amount of backup vocals together with Keith. As usual, the Stones went to the recording studio still hot off the road—the RCA studios in LA for the first time since 1966—to cut material for their next album *Emotional Rescue*. In October 1978, the Stones played in *Saturday Night Live*, their first major US television appearance since the *Ed Sullivan Show* in 1969.

On October 23, Keith's trial in Toronto got underway. Keith had started doing heroin again toward the end of the US tour, and he had lost 15 pounds since coming off the road. While the Crown sought jail term, the judge was more lenient and let him off for a benefit concert on behalf of the Canadian Institute for the Blind.[130] The other Stones stayed clear of Toronto.

One month later the Stones reconvened at Compass Point studios in Nassau to continue recording. Morals were down and bickering between Mick and Keith reached unprecedented levels. They did not speak with each other anymore, and they avoided each other in the studio, each working on separate days. Ronnie was heavy on drugs again, Bill threatened to quit, and Charlie told the press he was sick and tired of the whole thing. When Keith had been down with drugs, Mick had taken over the business. With Keith reasserting his role, Mick saw it "as a power grab" (Keith).[131]

---

129 Ibid., 306.

130 Rita Bedard, a blind girl from Canada, had followed the Stones for years, and Keith had arranged for her to travel with the band at no cost. Rumors are that Rita had lobbied the judge in person to let Keith off the hook.

131 Sandford, *Fifty Years*, 315.

It was solo career time again. Mick spent much time with the production of Peter Tosh's *Bush Doctor*, a Stones-financed release on Rolling Stones Records.[132] Ian put his own project together, *Rocket 88*, with the help of Charlie Watts. Departed Mick Taylor released a respectable but commercially unsuccessful solo album, spending the revenues on heroin. Ronnie released his own album *Gimme Some Neck*. Critics being positive, Ronnie put together a band, the New Barbarians, with Ian McLagan, Keith Richards, and Bobby Keys and toured the 18 cities in the United States for a month in April 1979, prefinanced by Columbia Records. The tour concluded with a live television special from LA Forum. Due to the band's enormous expenses (private Learjet, limos, drugs, and room service) Ron owed Columbia $200,000. On April 22, 1979, the New Barbarians performed the court-imposed benefit concert, 24 hours before the deadline. The concert was followed by the Stones performing their 78-tour set, voluntarily and at their own expense. The event generated $52,000 for the Canadian Institute for the Blind.

Back in Paris later in July, Keith recorded some 30 takes of a reggae song that would later evolve to "Start Me Up." The early reggae version was recently included on the bonus CD of the *Tattoo You* 40th anniversary reissue in November 2021. The Stones spent an enormous amount of time in Hollywood, the Bahamas, Paris, London, and New York on recording and overdubbing tracks for *Emotional Rescue*, one of their weaker albums (despite several good and innovative songs). The eponymous song is a very atypical recording written by Mick and inspired by the electronic music of Jean-Michel Jarre's *Oxygène*. Keith did not contribute to it. It was one of the instances where a conflict between Mick and Keith arose as to the musical direction of the Stones. Mick pushed for doing new things, whereas Keith objected. The album concluded with the bittersweet "All about You," the first of a series of remarkably moody compositions by Keith, who would perform them with an American crooner voice, a blend of Mississippi John Hurt and Tony Bennett. The song was neither about Keith's dog nor about Anita; it was about Mick. The critics hated the album; it nevertheless spent seven weeks at number one.

The band continued in hiatus. The New Barbarians performed in front of 250,000 people at Fort Knebworth, with Keith drinking more and more vodka, falling and shattering his nose. Ron worked on his next solo album; Bill produced the soundtrack for Ryan O'Neal's *Green Ice*, followed by his third

---

132 Bill had proposed to sponsor the joyful calypso musician Eddy Grant, but Mick and Keith preferred the more dark-toned Peter Tosh.

solo album (*Bill Wyman*). Mick traveled to Morocco from where he would send a telegram to Keith, scuppering plans for a 1980 Stones tour. "Mick waits until he's three thousand miles away and then he just sends a note, the old cunt" (Keith).[133] In December 1980, Mick spent six weeks on the set of Werner Herzog's *Fitzcarraldo* in the jungle of Lima, living in a mud-hut. While other actors wilted in the primitive living conditions, Mick remained imperturbable, finding humor even in the monkey that bit him. "Somehow, he constantly laughed in the face of adversity" (Werner Herzog). Mick could be vain, devious, and rude but also most charming. When BBC's Bob Harris ran four hours late for an interview blocked by heavy traffic, he was sweating bullets. To his surprise, Mick could not have been nicer when pouring the tea. "It was a bit like meeting the Queen" (Harris).[134]

In March 1981, Mick and Keith met in Barbados, where Bill Graham would propose his services for a tour, suggesting revenues of $22 million for twelve weeks' work. Mick let the band and their 70 tour employees know that he was ready "to put it all on the line" again.[135] However, things were again not rosy. Ron was so much on drugs that he was about to be replaced by Stevie Ray Vaughan or George Thorogood. Keith saved Ron's position by signing a formal tour rider guaranteeing that Ron would "not be found in possession of narcotics in any area, [or] be instantly suspended from his duties."[136] Ron needed the tour money badly. So did Bill, who had to finance two homes in England and France and the detox cure for his girlfriend in an expensive private clinic. Charlie struggled emotionally after the early death of his father and other family issues and started using alcohol, amphetamines, and even heroin. He was reluctant to go on tour. "Should I really tour? All that hassle. All that hard work. All those terrible arse-lickers. ... The only reason I could go through with it is that it's better than the fucking alternative" (Charlie).[137] Years later, Charlie stated in *Olé Olé* that he always considered rock stardom as "bullshit." Luckily, back in 1981, Charlie followed Keith's advice that going on stage is the best therapy. "You can be feeling like dog-shit, and within five minutes you're cured" (Keith).[138]

---

133 Sandford, *Fifty Years*, 320.
134 Ibid., 323.
135 Ibid., 324.
136 Ibid., 326.
137 Ibid., 327.
138 Ibid.

As much as one likes to think of a rock band as a brotherhood of eternal camaraderie, this is only true as long as the core performance is there and the members do not put the band at risk. Mick escaped at least three sacking attempts in the formative years (and a fourth attempt was considered later); Brian was sacked; Keith's replacement had been considered twice; and now Ronnie's. Only Charlie and Bill were never on the line, simply because whatever they did (if anything), it did not amount to a business threat.

Tattoo You was released in August 1981, while the band rehearsed for the tour on Long View Farm, a recording studio and the Stones' rehearsal facility located in the rolling hills outside Boston, Massachusetts. The Stones sent a roadie to buy 12 copies of the *New York Times*, which printed a raving review. Opening with "Start Me Up," transformed from a mellowish reggae tune into a powerful stadium anthem bearing Keith's signature open G tuning, it contained mostly rejects from recording sessions as old as 1972 and 1976, "retooled to 1981 specifications."[139] Departed Mick T. was surprised to hear his guitar solo on "Tops," recorded almost 10 years earlier. Similarly, the solo on "Worried About You" was from the auditioning sessions following the departure of Mick T., featuring Wayne Perkins.

The 1981 tour brought relief to the Stones' financial situation. It was a new kind of tour with the Stones enjoying a 90–10 cut with local promoters, merchandising (tongue-logoed T-shirts, socks, etc.), and a pay-per-view deal with HBO cable TV network for their Hampton, Virginia, show that grossed the Stones $3.2 million. Prince Rupert negotiated a side deal with Jovan Perfumes, which paid $4 million for having their name printed on the concert tickets. At that time rock had become a spectacle, and Mick wanted to be part of it. He unilaterally booked the biggest tour and invested in heavy sound and lighting equipment as well as in expensive purple and gold murals that would serve as stage backdrops. Mick recruited the Japanese stage designer Kazuhide Yamazaki for the design of their stadium-sized stages, which included runways and movable sections of the stage going out into the audience, as well as colored panels. Due to the size of the venues, the show had to use more visual gimmicks including pyrotechnics (fireworks) and lights. Charlie and Bill complained to Bill Graham that Mick had commissioned a million-dollar stage set, "and we're paying for it."[140]

---

139 Ibid.
140 Ibid., 329.

The 32-page tour contract to be signed by the Stones provided in Clause 9b that Mick should be "completely absent from the playing area" while Keith performed his three-minute solo vocal turn.[141] Mick and Keith had a tacit agreement never to venture into one another's quarters on Long View Farm. A reporter noticed that during the interview, Mick and Keith did not have much to say to each other. The other musicians referred to Mick as "Her Majesty." Getting the Stones to Long View Farm had been a problem in itself. Once reunited, Keith went off to stay at his friend's house in Florida. Bill was so furious that he flew home. When Keith returned from Florida, he was chronically late for everything and had to fly to Rome to get a new US work visa. Bill and Charlie were raging about all the delays. Once on tour, Ronnie and his friend Ian McLagan, hired as a keyboarder, were back on drugs. One night, Keith walked up to Ronnie's hotel room, a broken bottle in his hand. Both had to be separated after a punch-up. Hal Ashby, hired to shoot a concert movie, was carried out of the Stones' dressing room after overdosing on heroin. In another hotel, Keith would pull his gun and shoot a bullet through the floor, breaking up a party in the room beneath. Despite all these problems, the tour was a financial and artistic success. The Stones' fan base grew older and wealthier and was eager to pay 16 dollars for a ticket; tour director Bill Graham registered 2.5 million ticket applications and 4 million after he added 12 gigs to the tour. US Mail hired 245 part-time employees to process the ticket requests. Around 2.9 million people watched the shows, as many as came to see all their previous US tours together. Side acts included Prince, Iggy Pop, and Tina Turner. In Chicago, the Stones played in a small club with Muddy Waters, his last public appearance before his death. Each Stone would take some $5 million home, or $100,000 per concert, compared to $350 for the first US tour in 1964. It was exactly 20 years after Mick and Keith had met (again) at Dartford station. "They were on top of the world."[142]

Some critics alleged that the tour was for the money only and lacked any artistic enthusiasm. This is not entirely true. The opening, Glenn Miller followed by a fattened-up version of "Under My Thumb" (slouching speed, no minor chords, heavy organ, slow guitar interplay), is one of the best, but the rest does indeed not have the enthusiasm and energetic drive of the 1978 tour, which is even more noticeable as the set lists of both tours are significantly overlapping. Mick was back to androgyne with long hair; Keith smoked on

---

141 Ibid.
142 Ibid., 336.

stage like a docker; and Bill set new records in standing still and looking bored. Relations were down the sink. Mick and Keith regulated stage presence by contract and avoided each other during the tour. This does not necessarily reflect a problem, as a lengthy world tour requires space for privacy. Still, the atmosphere, characterized by excessive drug use, seems to have been rather on the dark side. While the 1978 tour had been labeled as the last, this 1981/1982 tour turned out to be the last tour before a hiatus of seven years. It could have been the very last.

6. Down in the Hole

In 1982, the Stones continued the tour in Europe. After seven years of service as a Stones secretary, Mick fired Jane Rose toward the end of 1981, after the end of the 1981 US tour and before the 1982 European tour. Keith immediately hired her as his personal assistant and manager, a move not appreciated by Mick. The Glimmer Twins would play 35 European shows between May and July 1982 without speaking to one another.

In spring 1982, the Stones had resumed their all-night long rehearsal pattern outside London. Photographer Gered Mankowitz was called for a shooting but had to come back twice only to find that Bill was absent. Mick assumed control of everything. He would sometimes leave the security area in disguise to watch the support act from among the audience. In Turin, the local security crew failed to recognize him and refused to let him backstage again. During the concert at Wembley Stadium, now released on the Deluxe Version of the *Tattoo You* anniversary release (November 2021), Keith forgot the riff of "She's So Cold." He was so angry at Woody for not covering him immediately that he punched him right in the face. At Naples airport, Keith and Charlie quarreled about who was going to get which seat on the plane. Privately, several Stones went through family and relationship trouble. Outside the concert, the Stones did not meet. "Socially, it was every man for himself" (Stu).[143]

The last concert of the tour in Leeds was officially released a few years ago as part of the *From the Vault* series. Depending on how you look at it, you see either a band in the state of fatigue (understandably, at the end of a tour) or a well-oiled rock 'n' roll machine, with a level of routine that allows for quasi-robotic playing. In fact, the band members looked detached and dressed down, with water bottles and cigarettes hanging from their guitar necks (more

---

143 Ibid., 338.

workmen convenience than rock 'n' roll attitude). Mick did his usual prancing around, but his facial expression was similarly robotic and emotionless. It is visually interesting how the Stones filled the space choreographically and geographically on a wider than ever stage, while remaining musically connected over large distances. Bill was standing motionless in a corner puffing his cigarettes and being ostensibly more bored than ever, and Ronnie was strolling around on the stage as if he were rehearsing his guitar parts in his garden at home.

In October 1982, the Stones began recording again in Paris for *Undercover*. Mick's reading of William Burroughs's *Cities of the Red Night* might have inspired some of the gore lyrics. Mick also proposed to reorganize recording practices and the songwriting system in what he described as a "more efficient way": songs should be written and finalized before the band walked into the studio. This would be a radical departure from Keith's habitual recording pattern (which happened to involve unpredictability in respect of timing and long waiting periods for the others). Mick also proposed to add modern production techniques such as sampling or phasing. Keith had other preferences ("You can overdo this streamlining shit"),[144] and he showed it by wearing a full-length black cape with a fedora in the studio, plus a sword stick on particularly stressful days. Mick asked Keith's guitar roadie Jim Barber to play a more "modern guitar" on *Too Much Blood*, "something like Andy Summers." In Sandford's words, "One aimed for timeliness, the other for timelessness."[145] *Undercover*, despite some remarkable tracks, turned out to be a technically good but artistically cold and unemotional album. There are some tracks on the B-side where even hardcore fans question their merit. In Julian Temple's video for the title song, Mick would be abducted by a Mexican-style gunman, whose leader, played by Keith, would blow Mick's brain out. The album hit number 11 in Britain and number 5 in the United States. It was the first commercial flop in 15 years.[146]

The Stones resumed their separately lived private lives. In February 1983, Mick accepted a £2 million advance from publisher Weidenfeld for writing his memoirs, but despite the help of technical assistant John Ryle, hired for £50,000, Mick could not remember anything noteworthy. As a last resort Mick approached Bill Wyman for support, as he was the band's archivist. Bill,

---

144 Ibid., 341.
145 Ibid.
146 Ibid., 346.

who was in the process of writing his own book, *Stone Alone*, told him to "get stuffed." Mick ultimately returned the advance and invested in some real estate in New York and a "shack" in Mustique.[147] Bill did write his book, Charlie bred horses, dogs, and sheep and played jazz. Charlie, Ronnie, and Bill collectively supported multiple sclerosis research as part of a supergroup with Eric Clapton, Jimmy Page, and Jeff Beck, as a tribute to the Faces' Ronnie Lane.

In August 1983, the Stones met in the Ritz in Paris to sign a new American distribution deal with CBS Records. The contract gave them $6 million each for 4 new albums, at that time the most lucrative in rock music history. CBS got the rights to the back catalog from *Sticky Fingers* onward. Mick Taylor was not part of the deal. The deal also included a proviso that CBS would release one or several solo albums by Mick. Keith may have overlooked that clause. Mick gave an eloquent speech on the occasion, which was typed up and distributed among the employees of CBS. "We are clearly living through one of the most difficult business cycles of recent times. Some say the record industry will pull out of the recession; others believe it's permanent. But I believe that CBS and the Stones will go forward to make some great music together. We're ready to roll."[148]

Around that time, Mick engaged in constant derogation of Keith who in turn would call Mick "Brenda the bitch." The Stones released only 40 minutes of music between November 1983 and August 1989. In May 1984, Mick began to record his first solo album, *She's the Boss*, with a plethora of guest musicians including Jeff Beck and namely synthesizer genius Jan Hammer; it turned out to be a *Miami Vice*–style album with many danceable and funky tracks, a remarkable product and agreeable to listen to, although slightly slick. During a meeting in the new Stones offices in Munro Terrace, Chelsea, on June 26, 1984, Mick told the other three attendees (excluding Ronnie) that he had plans for the rest of the year. There would be no Stones album or tour in 1984. Bill was displeased. "I've lost touch with whoever Mick is now. I'm sure he has as well."[149] It was not money Bill sought but mutual respect. In August 1984, four

---

147 The Caribbean island of Mustique had been purchased and developed by a relative of Prince Rupert, who also negotiated a beneficial tax status. In order to make the place attractive, the first lot was offered as a present to Princess Margaret. According to Prince Rupert, the acquisition of that shack was driven not so much by luxury taste but as part of an international tax strategy.

148 Sandford, *Fifty Years*, 347.

149 Ibid., 348.

Stones met for another business conference in Paris, Ronnie being on a detox cure. Mick declared that he now intended to tour behind his solo album. The only Stones output was a compilation under the title *Rewind* and a history video of the same name in which Mick and Bill would jointly present the band's history. When asked to explain the band's longevity, both answered as one: "Charlie Watts."[150]

Prince Rupert had convened the Stones for a business meeting in New York in October 1984 to talk about investments. The meeting was aborted when Keith arrived in the boardroom brandishing a ratchet knife, so much he was still annoyed about Mick's solo work. At the next meeting in Amsterdam, Keith made up for his appearance and took Mick out to get drunk. Back in the hotel at 5:00 a.m., Mick called Charlie's room and referred to him as "my drummer." Charlie got up, shaved, and dressed most elegantly, went to Mick's door, and punched him in the face. "Don't ever call me your drummer again. You're my fucking singer."[151] Keith was not pleased when Mick left the recording sessions to promote *She's the Boss* that was released on February 19, 1985: "Wimpy songs, wimpy performance, bad recording" (Keith).

Later that year the Stones reserved the new Pathé-Marconi studios in Rue de Sèvres to record music for their new album. Mick brought no material, and Keith arrived with 27 songs under titles like "Fight," "Had It with You," or "Knock Yer Teeth Out." Stu was to schedule the sessions such that the Glimmer Twins would not have to meet. Mick wanted the Stones to record in the way he had worked for his solo work with hired musicians, that is, everything had to be written out before a note would be played. One night the atmosphere exploded when Mick told Keith that he was tired of the ramshackle way the sessions were going. He listed several minutes of other shortcomings of the Stones' creative practice and summed it up with the words "We're just dicking around here." This view was not unanimously shared: "Jagger was around so infrequently, … it was just Charlie, Ronnie, Bill and me trying to make a record. It was very unprofessional, very stupid" (Keith). Although Mick postponed his solo tour, he rejected the idea of a Stones tour, characterizing them as a "bunch of pensioners" who were out of touch with the current music scene.[152]

150 Ibid., 350.
151 Ibid., 351.
152 Ibid., 353.

In July 1985, most of the Stones participated in Live Aid, but not together. Keith and Ronnie supported Bob Dylan, Mick performed a duet with David Bowie, "Dancing In the Street."

Later that summer, Ronnie mediated contacts between Mick and Keith. Just when tensions eased, Bill married an 18-year-old young woman after having dated her for several years, which raised a potential new legal threat. Charlie had problems at home and broke a leg falling down the stairs in his wine cellar. Most importantly, Stu died unexpectedly of heart failure in the waiting room of a doctor whom he intended to consult after having experienced respiratory trouble. This time, all the Stones came to the service. Keith embraced Mick and Woody: "Now who's gonna tell us off when we fuck up?"[153]

Dirty Work, the first album under the new contract, was released on March 24, 1986, after more than a year of work in three different cities. Most of the music was recorded by Keith, Ronnie, and Bill, together with other musicians. Charlie was mostly absent due to personal problems and replaced by studio musicians. Mick's vocals were added later. It is the first album on which Keith performs two vocal tracks. Keith was enthusiastic about the result and urged the band to tour behind it. Mick had his staff schedule a telephone conference with Charlie and Bill, only to talk about Keith. "We all do other things on the side—except him." Mick refused to go on tour with the Stones. He later claimed that "I was a hundred per cent right. It would have been the worst. Probably would have been the end of the band."[154] The album reached number three in Britain, number four in the United States. It was dedicated to Ian Stewart.

On April 24, Mick telegraphed Keith from Barbados that he would not have time for the Stones summer shows, as he planned to record his second solo album. When the Stones met on May 1 to cut a video for *Dirty Work*'s opening song "One Hit (To the Body)," nobody was speaking. Mick and Keith spent most of the shoot taking flying kicks at each other. Over the summer, all the Stones continued with solo projects. Bill mounted his solo band *Willy and the Poor Boys* (with Charlie or Ringo Starr on drums) and published a photo book about his Côte d'Azur neighbor Marc Chagall. Mick wrote the title song for Danny DeVito's *Ruthless People*; Charlie toured the United States with his 22-piece jazz band after finishing his detox. Keith engaged in a frenzy of dues-paying by supporting Etta James and Aretha Franklin, and he mounted several

---

153 Ibid., 356.
154 Ibid., 357.

shows with his mentor Chuck Berry, supported by former Allman Brother Chuck Leavell and Bobby Keys, captured in Taylor Hackford's documentary *Hail! Hail! Rock 'n' Roll*. Curiously, Chuck Berry would call Keith condescendingly Jack and would generally behave in quite a rude manner toward his disciple. Around that time, press reports about Bill's relationship triggered a wave of public outcry ("JAIL THIS WORM WYMAN").

On January 1, 1987, Mick rang Keith to wish him season's greetings, and Keith described their conversation as "very polite—very formal. He said that we must have a drink when we were back in New York." Nevertheless, *World War Three* (Keith) broke out on March 2, 1987, when Mick told the *Daily Mirror*, "I love Keith, I admire him, … ; but I don't feel we can really work together anymore."[155] Keith replied via the *Sun* that Mick "should stop trying to be like Peter Pan and grow up." Furious that Mick preferred "some little jerk off band" over the Stones, Keith tried to replace Mick by the Who's Roger Daltrey. Bill was quoted as calling Mick "the guilty one."

On July 17, 1987, Keith signed a contract with Virgin Records for two solo albums and started auditioning musicians at the Hit Factory in New York, while Mick was across Broadway at Right Track Studios mixing *Primitive Cool* and dress rehearsing his delayed tour. Mick was keen on having Jeff Beck in the tour band, but the latter declined; the money offered by Mick was too low. "It was laughable … an insult. I'd love to play with the old geezer, but I can't believe how tight he is."[156] *Primitive Cool* hit number 41 in America and number 19 in Britain. On October 19, 1987, the Dow Jones crashed. Three days later, the album had dropped from the charts. But for the Wall Street crash, the band might have followed Prince Rupert's reported advice to quietly fold things up. But now "one of the Rolling Stones began calling the others to talk about putting the band back together. It was Mick Jagger."[157]

What started as personal tension between two idiosyncratic and very different (albeit complementary) individuals escalated to a conflict about band strategy. Mick's proposal to "modernize" recording technique may have killed the unique feature that singled out the Stones methodology of making albums from that of most other bands: the relentless fine-tuning and polishing of the final recording. To give a concrete example: Would Mick's proposed methodology have left us with the early version of "Start Me Up," rather than the later

155 Ibid., 362.
156 Ibid., 364.
157 Ibid.

glorious stadium anthem that had such a great career? On the other hand, Keith's totally bohemian way demanded a lot from his fellow band members. Another question is whether Mick really believed in good faith that his proposal was the way of the future or whether he knew that it was unacceptable to Keith and launched it for the purpose of provoking a chain reaction. There may not be a clear answer to these questions. The subtext of Mick's message was that he no longer enjoyed spending time with the boys. A fact is that Mick had just completed his first "modern style" solo effort, but while it earned praise from critics, it did not sell. Another fact is that individuals, even where they are members of the same band, continue to have different emotional and social needs. One person may need more proximity and another person may need more distancing, and there is no right or wrong. All that matters is whether there is a sufficient level of self-awareness and restraint to make the "working together" work.

The overall situation at that time, however, had worsened compared to earlier crises. The feuds in the mid-1970s had been between Mick and Keith only; now they infected the entire band. Or almost. In fact, there is no information about Ron ever being frustrated. With his naturally good mood, he continued to mediate between Mick and Keith when even Charlie no longer had the nerve to do this. Ronnie excelled in mediating, both because of his character and because he badly needed the Stones to survive to earn a living. So much for the band members. If at that stage Prince Rupert, the financial architect and father figure of the Stones, recommended winding down the band, the Stones must have been on the very edge of breakup.

Had the story ended there, the Stones would still be a good memory for the older fans, just like Procol Harum or Jefferson Airplane. However, they would not have achieved the status of intergenerational blues-rock prophets that teach music, joy, and words of wisdom to millions of fans of all ages.

Part Three—Turning Gold into Riches (1989 to Date)

1. Bigger Than Us

On May 18, 1988, all four Stones met in the same room for the first time in two years. Mick proposed to tour, but it was now Keith who refused; he had made commitments to tour behind his solo album *Talk Is Cheap* with his own band, the X-Pensive Winos. After a daylong debate, the Stones agreed to a full-scale come back in 1989. Mick was confident the demographics were right for a tour. At this point, Keith said to Brenda-Mick, "Listen, darling, this thing is bigger than both of us. Capisce?"[158]

This May 18, 1988, meeting was probably the single most important business meeting the band ever held. It was in a certain way more important than the founding of the band itself. Not only had the original founding of the band in 1962 been an informal process rather than a constitutional act, but it was a decision about launching an amateur musical venture for a short period of time not expected to last more than two years. By 1988, the Stones had already achieved a globally unequaled status as veteran rock rebels with a great musical legacy measurable impact on society. They were influencers way beyond their musical work product. If the band had dissolved at this point, it would have meant putting an end to an unprecedented accumulation of tangible and intangible assets, goodwill, and fame. The Stones could already have claimed to be one of the longest lasting rock acts, certainly longer that Cream, Deep Purple, Led Zeppelin, the Beatles, and many others. However, what happened at this business meeting was a leap to a higher level of both professionalism and consciousness. Up to that point, the individual band members—at least Mick and Keith—had operated as a true band with residues of an individualistic mindset. In the May 1988 meeting, Keith put on the table what seems to be a first-time proposition: this is bigger than us. This "bigger than us" is a qualitative leap forward in the band's collective self-awareness and significantly reinforced the cement which had held the band together ever since. As the story will unfold, it is not that they had less interpersonal tensions or a lesser need to express their individuality through personal projects outside the Stones. However, they acknowledged that the Stones had by now a personality of its own, like a corporate entity or a legal person. "The Rolling Stones" was no longer a loose association of the members but a distinct persona with a separate personality that had either developed out of its own making or,

---

158 Ibid., 367.

alternatively, been bestowed upon it by others: by fate, God, the public, or a mix of all. Over the years, comments by the band members emphasized the theme of "reception," meaning that they received ideas from the outside, transformed them musically, and passed them on to their audience. This new awareness made it easier for the band members to get through the coming several decades together. Admittedly, the enormous financial success may also have helped. Was it the driver? Probably not. Many people aspire to be rich but few succeed. People would not put up money for concert tickets just to enrich the band members. They pay to see the sparks fly. They must be satisfied, because they come back ever since.

It was in that second part of their career that the Stones designed the giant tours grossing hundreds of millions, attended by millions of viewers, with an ever-increasing sophistication in merchandising and other accessory revenue streams. It was a redemptive moment not only for the band but for the existing and future fan community too. Many of today's younger enthusiastic fans were not even born then. For professionals in working life the Stones are no longer just a group of musically gifted hedonistic rebels but "pillars of society" from whom we can learn how to make a successful business grow and last. They teach us virtues such as creativity, innovation, perseverance, endurance, discipline, professionalism, camaraderie, and passion. Most importantly they teach us the benefit of a zest of self-derision and the importance of empathy and compassion. In the Spielberg movie *Terminal*, there is a key scene where a senior member of some airport surveillance authority comes to inspect the airport and is shown around by the young overambitious airport director. When the latter mentions the problem of the irregular passenger ("against the rules"), the senior member admonishes him with the words "Don't forget compassion. It is all this country is about."

Reconciliation made slow progress. Keith was not yet ready to record with Mick but accepted the idea of taking a long view of their partnership of almost 30 years. "Ninety-nine per cent of the male population would give a limb to live like him. To be Mick Jagger. ... And he's not happy. I'm trying to grow the thing up, and I'm saying we don't need the lemon-yellow tights and the cherry picker to make a good Stones show. There's a more mature way of doing it." At the Hit Factory, Keith played his new album to his guests. Returning from the bathroom, he glimpsed Mick dancing away to the music. Keith retraced his steps, coughed, and walked in to find Mick sitting on a sofa pretending to read the *New York Times*.

Talk Is Cheap was released on October 4, 1988. Mick, who had already toured Japan in March (the "Suntory Dry Beer Live Mick Jagger Experience in Japan" tour), played another 18 concerts in Australia and Indonesia. Keith commented harshly on his band to the press. Mick replied that Keith was just trying to get publicity for his own record. "It was the only way he could get any. He takes things more personally. He's had a more problematic life."[159] On November 24, 1988, Keith embarked on a three-week American tour with his band. At the same time, Prince Rupert was working on a $70 million deal to get the Stones back on the road.

In February 1989, Mick and Keith met in Barbados to record songs in Eddy Grant's Blue Wave Studios. Keith was "thrilled to bits" to be there but also wary of working with Mick, relaunching the Stones in the era of Guns N' Roses and Nirvana. He told his family that he would be back either in two weeks or two days. This time, the Glimmer Twins wasted no time. Each had brought surplus material from his solo work and "juices flowed under the tropical sun."[160] Within a weekend, they had three tracks done.

In early 1989, Prince Rupert received a phone call from Michael Cohl, a tour promoter. Cohl had handled some Stones gigs in Canada on behalf of Bill Graham. He was nicknamed "the Howard Hughes of rock and roll." Cohl proposed his services ($40 million for 40 shows), but Prince Rupert warned him that they were about to sign with Bill Graham. Cohl replied, "I am prepared to pay you twice as much." Mick was initially reluctant, because the Graham team had a good understanding of his ideas in terms of scenery, stage design, and production value. Cohl brought stage experts Peter Mensch and Cliff Burnstein in, and that turned Mick around. Prince Rupert arrived with New York attorney John Branca, who convinced the Stones of the merits of centralizing their ticket sales, retail spin-offs, and other logistics under a single supremo, a system that had worked well for Branca's other client, Michael Jackson. Historically, the band would hire a tour director who would call on local promoters in each city to set up shows. "Individual deals would have to be cut with each promoter, who took, say, 10% to 15% of ticket sales after the cost of the show. The tour director would then have to collect $250,000 here, $400,000 there, from promoters all over."[161] By cutting out Bill Graham and going with Toronto-based Michael Cohl, who in turn oversaw a sponsorship deal with Budweiser and assorted TV and merchandising rights, the

---

159 Ibid., 368–9.

160 Ibid., 372.

161 Andy Serwer, Julia Boorstin, and Ann Harrington, "Inside the Rolling Stones Inc," *Fortune Magazine*, September 30, 2002.

deal guaranteed the Stones net profits of $18 million each for a 15-week tour. Cohl "would also produce new streams of revenue by selling skyboxes, bus tours, and TV deals, and by taking merchandising to a new level. He would bring in corporate sponsors like Volkswagen and Tommy Hilfiger. And most important, he would help stitch these operations together, through cross-promotion and the like, to maximize their earning power" (Serwer). When Keith returned, it was merely to pack.

The decision to depart radically from an established and successful way of touring was neither taken lightheartedly nor was it risk-free: having signed up with the Stones as tour director, Cohl had to deal with the fact that he did not have the $40 million he had promised to the band, but he eventually managed to get the money. Another complicating factor was that for the business model to pass muster, the band members had to pass successfully life insurance medicals. Moreover, Cohl did not have relevant experience: "I think Michael would admit that it was a huge learning curve for him doing Steel Wheels. Michael had never done it before really, so it was a bit of a gamble" (Jagger).[162]

On January 18, 1989, Mick and Keith made their first public appearance together in three years, when Pete Townshend introduced the Stones into the Rock and Roll Hall of Fame, joined for the occasion by Ron and Mick Taylor. After Pete's speech, Mick thanked everyone saying, "We're not quite ready to hang up the number yet." The three Stones and Mick Taylor jumped on stage to perform "Satisfaction," joined by Pete, Bruce Springsteen, and Stevie Wonder. "Suddenly the dysfunctional, wheezing geezers were transformed back in to the greatest band in the world."[163]

In February, the five Stones reunited in Barbados for the first proper Stones sessions in four years. For the next six weeks, the Stones churned out a full album, *Steel Wheels*, to support their upcoming tour. In May, the Stones finished the album in the Olympic Studios, the first time after they had used it for *Beggar's Banquet*. Mick also met with Michael Cohl. Cohl's first coup for the Stones was a deal with Event Transportation System (ETS), a Canadian firm that resold concert tickets at up to five times face value as part of a VIP experience. ETS guaranteed Cohl and the band $625,000, and Mick and Keith received a further share of the profits. Bill Graham was unhappy. It "was like watching my favorite lover become a whore." He managed to come up with a counteroffer that guaranteed the Stones marginally less upfront but a greater

---

162 Ibid.
163 Sandford, *Fifty Years*, 372.

potential payday from back-end rights to the various concert movies and merchandising. Bill pitched the project to Mick on a Concorde flight to New York and asked Mick, "After all this time, what's really the difference to you guys between sixteen million dollars and eighteen million?" Mick's reply was unambiguous. "Two million bucks, Bill."

For the first time, all five Stones were regularly punctual at the studio. It was "much more of a drill than before" (Mick). The atmosphere was good. Keith, long known as the "temperamental genius" of the band, was now affectionately promoted to "the madman." By June, the Stones' organization with 370 employees was putting together a piece of rock theater to be pumped out on vast futuristic looking stages. The set was of such extravagant size that it did not fit in some arenas. The tower from which Mick sang needed flashing red lights on top in order to warn passing jets. Ronnie was eventually promoted to equity partner. Mick and Keith took a short trip to Morocco to record some pipes and drum music with the same local Joujouka musicians that Brian had recorded 20 years earlier. CBS lived up to its commitments by strongly supporting the new album. On July 11, the Stones showed up at New York Central Station to announce their 11th US tour. One reporter asked whether they were doing it for the money. "What about love?" Mick asked back. Keith took the mike and said, "It's for the glory, darling. The glory."[164]

From the beginning, business was brisk. Four shows at Shea Stadium sold out overnight and two in Toronto in six hours. One block of 200,000 seats was sold via phone at 2,000 per minute. From time to time, the old tensions would reappear. When Keith disliked the horn section, he called Bobby Keys who was still under a ban, having been expelled during the 1973 tour for running up a massive champagne bill in a Frankfurt hotel that exceeded his entire tour salary (heroin use on tour may also have been a factor). Keith told Bobby to fly over and hide away when arrived. He made Bobby appear as a surprise at the time of rehearsing "Brown Sugar," Mick commenting "What the fuck … ," (reportedly he would not speak to Bobby for the next year). Mick also unsuccessfully tried to eject Jane Rose from the touring family. Toward the end of the rehearsals, and at Keith's displeasure, Mick introduced keyboarder Matt Clifford, who was supposed to give the Stones a more modern sound. Keith also opposed some of the lavish concert accessories. When Mick suggested bringing in a click-in track to get the tempos right, Keith objected: "I'll

---

164 Ibid., 376.

handle the tempos, mate."[165] Mick jogged seven miles every day with a professional coach while Keith trained on vodka and cigarettes. All Stones passed the pre-tour physical tests required by the insurers. On August 12, the band gave the first American concert in 8 years in front of 200 people. *Steel Wheels* was released a week later. The album was made at wild speed, and there was no time for artwork. Critics were mixed. The album hit number two in Britain and number one in the United States.

On August 31, 1989, a 60-strong police motorcycle escort drove the Stones to Philadelphia's Veteran Stadium for their first paying concert in 7 years. It was a total success. With the *Steel Wheels* tour, the Stones had reached a new level of professionalism. Groupies were replaced by wives and kids; Mick used a preshow meditation zone with Buddhist icons; Keith and Ronnie bothered tuning their guitars before going on stage; and the operation ran like a mobile company. There were no less than 15 musicians on stage, including a 5-piece horn section, 3 backing singers, and two keyboard players, all in all a well-rehearsed show band. When the Stones went backstage, it was into a hamlet of individual changing suites, children's nurseries, buffets, bars, games rooms, and a communal lounge equipped with Persian rugs, couches, and a fireplace. The music and the show, it was all "fucking immense" (Charlie).[166]

In Toronto, Keith discovered that some roadies had eaten his personal preconcert shepherd's pie. The band's longtime assistant Tony King had to tell Mick that Keith refused to go on stage until he had had his pie. With 53,000 people waiting in the arena, the pie had to be brought to the arena by the police. Four sold-out shows at the LA Coliseum followed, with Guns N' Roses opening for the Stones. The Stones also played an unscheduled gig in Atlantic City, after Donald Trump had offered them $6 million to do so, with Axl and Slash and Eric Clapton and John Lee Hooker as guest stars.[167] After four months and sixty shows, three-and-a-half million customers had been to the show, and the tour grossed $98 million in ticket sales and $40 million in merchandising. It was the most lucrative tour ever. In total, the *Steel Wheels* tour made over $260 million worldwide, a record for a rock tour at that time. *Steel*

---

165 In most bands, everybody follows the drummer. In the Stones, the late Charlie followed Keith.

166 Sandford, *Fifty Years*, 380.

167 This concert was broadcasted in digital quality and was available for some time on three CDs as a lawful bootleg recording in Europe in the early 1990s due to a temporary loophole in European copyright law.

Wheels became the template for the subsequent tours, the business model being refined gradually.[168]

There were still traces of the old feud. Keith disliked the ritual of shaking hands with beer executives, dubbing Mick a "smart little motherfucker." The touring family had been quickly divided into Mick's camp and Keith's camp, each observing the moves of the other. Despite Keith's criticism, Mick played more and more guitar onstage, and his private tuning room was quickly christened the "House of God." Bill Graham noted that the "singing businessman" had set the tone that had created the tensions. "But there was another side to Mick that made him a considerable figure and accounts for the Stones surviving all the pitfalls. ... He saw the band through one crisis after another."

The European "Urban Jungle" tour in summer 1990 was also a success, despite the scaled down stage set. In London, old Dartford friend Derek Taylor asked Mick whether his Pretty Things could open for the Stones. While awaiting Mick's answer, he noticed that Mick spoke to the press about the "constant shit" of reliving the past. His premonition proved right. A young band named Gun opened for the Stones. The Stones also played in Prague at the personal invitation of Václav Havel. The Australian leg planned for late summer was canceled due to travel hassles and general burnout. In October 1990, the Stones met for a forward-planning meeting, and Bill announced that he was considering quitting. One of the reasons given was that he had developed a fear of flying. Bill aired other long-standing artistic grievances. "Fuck you lot, you didn't use any of my songs." Keith replied, "Haven't you sussed that they're useless songs?"[169]

2. Problems Solved?

Throughout 1991, 1992, and 1993, the Stones lived their private lives, only meeting to cut a single-supported anti-gun video "Highwire," one of the very few political songs, following the beginning of the first Gulf War. Bill refused to appear in the video. For the single's B-side, the Stones wrote a James Brown–style song called "Sex Drive". In February, the Stones cashed in $5 million for letting "Satisfaction" appear in a Snickers advertisement. With the quite unexciting live album called *Flashpoint*, the Stones delivered their fourth and

---

168 Andy Serwer et al., "Inside the Rolling Stones Inc."
169 Sandford, *Fifty Years*, 386.

final piece to CBS, which would soon be sold to Sony. Quite quickly Richard Branson offered $45 million if the Stones signed up a deal with Virgin Music.

In early 1992, Mick participated in the creation of Britain's National Music Day, for which he performed at Hammersmith Odeon with Charlie and Ron. On a trip to Tokyo to promote his (unsuccessful) movie *Freejack*, he was intercepted at Narita Airport as a "social deviant" and "convicted drug felon" and interrogated for five hours. Mick was cleared after two days and finally allowed to enter Japan. While Mick was working with young hip-hop producer Rick Rubin, Keith joined Bob Dylan for a concert in Sevilla. When asked why Dylan would rearrange his hits in an unrecognizable format, Keith replied, "Because he's a cunt."[170] Charlie went back to his farm after wrapping up his Charlie Parker jazz project; Bill ran his burger restaurant called Sticky Fingers and continued to insist that he would leave the Stones. Keith noted, "I reckon he's on his third menopause."[171] Mick built a home studio in his French castle to record songs for his excellent, quite spiritual but low selling album *Wandering Spirit* (to be released on February 9, 1993), and Keith worked on his second solo album *Main Offender*. The album was released in October 1992 to warm reviews and tepid sales.[172] Ron put on heavily criticized art exhibitions in London, Dublin, and Tokyo and had difficulties in finding a record company for his next solo album *Slide on This*. The very respectable and musically diverse album was finally released on New Jersey–based Continuum Records in late 1992, and it did not enter the charts. Ron, however, managed to sell a painting portraying the Stones in a Jacobean interior for $1.2 million. Charlie toured the United States in his three-piece with a large jazz band and was invited to appear as musical guest on David Letterman's *Late Night Show*. This would have exposed the album to an audience of six million potential customers, but according to NCB rumors Charlie had to be accompanied by the show's in-house band. "Minutes before the programme's scheduled air-time, he left the building with a muttered 'Fuck it' and wandered off into the warm New York night."[173] Keith toured the United States with his X-Pensive Winos, playing fantastic concerts in mostly smaller venues. None of these extracurricular activities ever created a question mark as to the continued existence of the

---

170 Ibid., 391.
171 Ibid., 392.
172 Ibid., 394.
173 Ibid., 395.

Stones. During the whole period, neither Mick nor Keith ever threatened to leave the Stones.

It is interesting to see how individual projects fused after a period of intense and successful group activity. Tour life imposed heavy constraints on the individual, and the individual members needed time to breathe. With the tour experience being financially rewarding and altogether pleasant, there was no more need to view solo adventures with suspicion.

In the meantime, Branson had signed the Stones to a £30 million contract with a guaranteed upfront payment of £4.5 million for each of the band's next three albums. Virgin Records got the rights (including the publishing rights) for the back catalog since *Sticky Fingers*. The deal was limited to audio rights (not visual rights), and it was signed by Mick, Keith, and Charlie only. Concurrently with the Virgin deal, the Stones discontinued Rolling Stones Records. Three months later, Branson sold Virgin Music to Thorn EMI for $1 billion, the most ever paid for an independent company in England with recorded posttax earnings of £500,000 and assets worth £3 million. Richard Branson used the money to start Virgin Airlines. EMI released *Jump Back*, another compilation of hits from 1971 to date.

For years after *Steel Wheels*, Mick and Keith would meet in Mick's New York home to exchange *stuff* that each of them had come up with. Keith realized that all ingredients for a new chapter in the Stones history were present. "What we need to do is to focus."[174] It was only at that time that Bill Wyman announced his departure publicly. Keith called Bill, saying, "You're walking away from millions of quid." Alas, Bill had other things on his plate. It was the third team change in 31 years. Fans were speculating that the Stones would bring Mick Taylor back and switch Ronnie to bass, but this did not happen. In the words of Tome Keylock, "The Stones don't give a shit. It's like the Mafia. They never forget who's crossed them and, once you do, there's no way back." When the Stones auditioned replacements for Bill, they surprised the candidates by playing "Beast of Burden" at half speed. After several rounds of auditioning, the Stones hired Darryl Jones, a funk-rock jazzman who had played with Miles Davis. He would earn $200,000 per tour. Observers noted the change in sound this hire would bring about. The artist formerly known as Prince once observed that Jones had turned the Stones into a funk band.

Bill Wyman's departure is one of the most intriguing moments in the history of the Stones. First, Bill is one of the most interesting rock bassists of all

---

174 Ibid., 396.

times. One can listen repeatedly to Stones albums just focusing on the bass line without getting bored. This is even more telling as Keith had a tendency of pushing Bill's bass back in the final mix so that one has to stretch one's ear to actually hear it. Whenever one hears the bass distinctly, there is a significant likelihood that Keith or Ronnie played it. Their bass style is musically less intriguing. Keith plays the bass more like a guitar (e.g. "Before They Make Me Run"), and a saying from the *Circus* project goes that Keith needs to show the world that he plays the bass as well as Jack Bruce. Bill once explained that all he did on stage was "to fatten up the music" and that is exactly what he did. It is somewhat true that since his departure, the bass lines are no longer intriguing. If he plays at all on album tracks, Darryl Jones is somewhat overqualified for the job in a rock band, and on stage he looks almost as disengaged as Bill did before. The artist formerly known as Prince was right: the departure of Bill changed the Stones' musical style more than the departure of Mick Taylor or Brian.

Most curiously, one would expect Bill, pre- and post-departure, to excel in playing great bass lines and put them forward in the mix of his solo albums. Not surprisingly, the bass is distinctly audible in the mix on his solo albums, including the pre-departure albums on which he proved his songwriting capabilities with beautifully constructed songs. However, most of the time the bass lines on Bill's solo albums are not that exciting. Changed interpersonal dynamics may explain this phenomenon. Whatever we do, we are best when part of a challenging team where every member is the other members' critic and editor and thereby causes each team member to anticipate the critical reaction of the others to each contribution made. The more this team constraint triggers a frustration of the self, the more it pushes the band member to excel. On the other hand, once the team member is free from this constraint, the tension drops and so does the quality of the individual output. The Beatles are the best example of this effect. As long as they were a band, John and Paul edited each other and both contributed great songs. Once they went solo, they did whatever they want. The overall quality of their production was not at the previous level, as is the case for Mick and Keith. This phenomenon is exacerbated where the musicians involved are not a true band but just hired session men.

During this whole period, the Stones recorded music in Barbados, Dublin, New York, and Hollywood for their upcoming album *Voodoo Lounge*. Mick had invited producer Don Was to mix the recordings. When Don arrived at the studio, Keith told him that he was not needed. Don left but was called back two days later by Mick. He finally coproduced the album. Was noticed that the Stones did not communicate with each other during the endless jam sessions, and he spent much time trying to make sense of the cryptic instructions Mick, Keith, or Charlie would give him. He thought they planned the sessions when he was not around, but they did not. Each of the Stones had his own ideas for the album's sound. Mick wanted a hip album with "groove, African licks and stuff"; Keith wanted "Elvis vibe"; and Charlie wanted the drums louder in the mix.[175]

On May 3, 1994, the Stones met in New York to announce their 12th American tour. In the press conference, Mick said, "We're still a fucking good band." As usual, the Stones moved the rehearsals to Toronto, one reason being that they only had US working visas for six months and wanted to limit their stay in the United States to a minimum for fiscal reasons. For the rehearsals, a crew member would play the selected song on a CD, with Keith and Ronnie playing along while Mick would read the lyrics from a songbook. Within minutes, the energy was there. Saxophonist Bobby Keys, keyboarder Chuck Leavell, Lisa Fischer and Bernard Fowler (two backup singers, who had worked with the Stones and their members since the mid-1980s, and Bernard still does today), plus a horn section, would give the Stones the full showband sound. Matt Clifford was not re-invited. At the same time, Mark Fisher worked on the latest state-of-the-art stage for a cost of $3 million. It included a towering bazaar with two mainframe computers for the lighting instructions, a 90-ton sound system, and 300-foot-long banks of video screens, plus a fire-spewing steel arch known as *the Cobra*. The *Voodoo Lounge* tour would travel during 13 months through 25 countries. The tour was managed by Michael Cohl following the all-in model of the *Steel Wheels* tour, with the one important difference that it guaranteed the Stones even higher profits. Michael Cohl's memo to the personnel from October 5, 1994 stated, "The main benign messages we need to disseminate are 1) sell the remaining tickets, 2) publicize the pay per view; 3) generate merchandising awareness ... All [other] considerations should be tied to these three points."[176]

The *Voodoo Lounge* album was released in July 1994, and the tour started on August 1. Again, the Stones would include some never-performed live rarities in the set list. With 55,000 spectators paying an average of $60 each, the expensive stage was paid for after the first night. An hour before each concert there was a meet-and-greet session with Budweiser representatives, and

---

175 An unofficial set of bootleg recordings (*The Voodoo Sessions*, 12 CDs) tracks the creative process in fascinating detail: at the beginning, endless and repetitive jams with just Keith and Charlie, that slowly develop into full structured songs.

176 Sandford, *Fifty Years*, 404.

half an hour before the concert Keith and Ronnie would retire to their tuning room while the backstage area was cleared of all "non-essential personnel." A total of eight million spectators would attend the tour, of which three million in the United States. Ticket sales, merchandising sales including a jacket for $525, and pay-per-view TV-specials generated unprecedented levels of return (Mick and Keith also appeared on *Beverly Hills, 90210*, a move to familiarize the younger generations with the older band). Even the Stones' wives and friends admitted backstage with VIP passes had to pay for them. For the US leg alone, each Stone took home $19 million, the fruit of four-and-a-half months of work. It was around that time that Nicky Hopkins and Jimmy Miller died at age 50 and 52 respectively. The South American and Asian legs were also successful. A concert in Beijing was canceled by the authorities for reasons of "cultural pollution" and the risk of traffic jams. Volkswagen sponsored the European tour with a $10 million grant and launched a special version of the Golf with the Rolling Stones' *Voodoo Lounge* symbol on the rear and the tongue stitched into the seat fabric. All 39 European concerts were sold out in record time. It was a fantastic success, financially and artistically.

As soon as the tour was over, Michael Cohl started to work on the next tour. Meanwhile, Microsoft paid $5 million for the right to use "Start Me Up" in an advertising. Mick and Keith declined a $2 million offer to write music for the next James Bond film. In 1996, Allen Klein released the CD and DVD versions of *The Rolling Stones Rock and Roll Circus*. None of the band attended the launch event. At that time, Mick incorporated his own movie production company *Jagged Films* and bought the rights to Robert Harris's novel *Enigma*, which Tom Sheppard would adapt to screen. Keith returned to his Jamaican home to record reggae roots gospels with local musicians under the name of *Wingless Angels*.

3. Back to Zero?

When Keith called for a band meeting in New York in January 1997, the tension was back right away. Mick wanted to focus on films and solo records rather than "turning in to a fucking oldies jukebox." He also found it too early to restart again. The Virgin representatives insisted on the need to maintain market shares and rework the proven album-tour-video formula. When Michael Cohl outlined another $300 million project that guaranteed each of the Stones $35 million, Mick finally gave in. Soon afterward Mick and Keith moved to Barbados to write and record songs for a new album. Again Mick wanted to give the music a modern sound and hired hipsters like Danny Saber (Busta

Rhymes and Black Grape) and the Dust Brothers (Beastie Boys and Beck) to coproduce the album, all "techno geeks" and "knob-twiddlers" in Keith's eyes. When Keith bumped into Kenny "Babyface" Edmonds in the control room one night, he said, "You cut with Mick, your face is gonna look like mine. You may be Babyface now but you're gonna be Fuckface after you're done with that guy."[177] By late June, Keith and Mick would work on their contributions to the album in different rooms and towns and with different crews. Mick worked with Danny Saber and Matt Clifford, Keith with ex–Beach Boy Blondie Chaplin,[178] the Wino's Waddy Wachtel and hired Jeff Sarli (Bluesiana, Marshall Crenshaw) to play some rockabilly-bass stomp. Mick and Keith agreed over the phone to change the album title from *Blessed Poison* to *Bridges to Babylon*, and they agreed on the artwork for the album cover. On June 30, Don Was reported the completion of the album. The next morning he had Mick on the phone complaining that Keith had been given three songs on the album (compared to the usual one or two), which he deemed "unheard of" and "unacceptable." Was recalled, "It was a total standoff between these two guys, neither one was backing down, and we were going to miss the release date and the tour was going to start without a new album out there." An engineer resolved the issue by editing out the space between the two final songs of the album, both sung by Keith, which as a result became a medley. Mick finally agreed. When Keith listened to the finished album one month later, his daughter Angela noted that Mick's (fantastic) contribution "Anybody Seen My Baby" had been unconsciously inspired by K. D. Lang's "Constant Craving." Keith called Mick and, with the help of some attorneys, a solution was negotiated with K. D. Lang and her songwriting partner Ben Mink. Both received credits and royalties. Keith made sure the money came out of Mick's share.[179]

Bridges to Babylon was released on September 29, 1997 and sold six million copies during the two years of the *Bridges to Babylon* tour, which had started on September 23 in Chicago. The tour was artistically fantastic, with several early songs performed live for the first time, and the stage was "a hi-tech marvel that

---

177 Ibid., 409.

178 Since the *Bridges to Babylon* tour in 1997, Blondie is part of the Stones' touring family. Standing next to Lisa and Bernard, he sings and discreetly plays acoustic and electric guitar to support Keith. Some fans complain that they do not want to pay expensive concert tickets to "hear Blondie Chaplin play Satisfaction."

179 Sandford, *Fifty Years*, 410.

resembled something out of a biblical epic shot in Las Vegas" (Sandford).[180] For the first time, the Stones rehearsed some 30 songs that spectators could vote in over the internet, thereby influencing the set list and resulting in different set lists in different venues. Telecoms giant Sprint had replaced Budweiser as tour sponsor, which did not prevent Keith form telling the press that he rarely used a mobile phone because "the fuckers give you cancer." The US leg of the tour ended with a concert filmed in Saint Louis for release on a DVD. After 12 weeks of touring, the Stones had generated $89 million, with another $200 million to follow. The ticket prices for good seats were upped to $300 and $500 for the show in Las Vegas' Hard Rock Casino. "It's only money," Mick would observe. On the side, Prince Rupert brokered a deal with Pepsi Cola. The company paid $4 million for a private concert in Honolulu and $2 million for the right to use "Brown Sugar" in an advertising. The tour went to South America and even Moscow, where Keith invented his signature greeting "Great to be here. Great to be anywhere." Only the home front had to suffer. Four UK shows were canceled after the Labour Government introduced new tax rules according to which expatriate Britons lost their tax-exempt status if they did work of any kind while physically located in the UK. Other gigs in Europe had to be canceled for a variety of reasons. The tour closed in September 1998 with a concert in Istanbul.

On November 2, 1998, the Rolling Stones released *No Security*, a strangely forceless compilation of those rarely performed live songs that do not make a good live album when put together. Deviating from the usual pattern, the Stones went back to touring in January 1999 to support that live album. The *No Security* tour encompassed 34 gigs in the United States, all of which were deliberately designed as indoor events. A second *Bridges to Babylon* tour comprising eleven shows in Europe made up for those shows that had to be canceled during the first round. In London, the Stones played in Shepherd's Bush in front of less than 2,000 people.

At the end of the 1990s, the Stones had beaten all records in terms of fame, artistic achievements, social status, and financial success. At the age of 56, Mick Jagger remained convinced that the Stones' creative and commercial peak lay ahead of them. "You either keep moving, or you die."[181]

---

180 Ibid., 412.
181 Ibid., 421.

4. Into a New Millennium

For the Stones, the new millennium began with a joint appearance by Mick and Keith in Madison Square Garden as part of the Concert for New York City organized after the 9/11 events. Together, they performed "Salt of the Earth" from the 1968 album *Beggar's Banquet*. Keith changed the original lyrics from "Raise your glass to the good and the evil" to "Raise your glass to the good, not the evil." Otherwise, both were again in a period of noncommunication. Keith was eager to tour but Mick focused on his movies and his new solo album *Goddess in the Doorway*, a spiritually charged album released on November 19, 2001. Appraised by the critics, Keith called it "dogshit."

At that time, both Mick and Keith were further developing their personal image: Keith as the truthful and impetuous rock and roll buccaneer and Mick as the serious businessman with a busy professional and private life. In spring 2000, Mick spoke at his old school in Dartfort after donating money for the school's new swimming pool. "As Mick got up to speak ... it suddenly struck home that the guiding theme of his discourse was how it all had been accidental. There was no moral to his story except how easily it could have been otherwise" (Sandford). Soon after, in May 2000, Mick's mother died at age 87. Friends say that with her combination of self-discipline, charm, and dogged social ambition, she had been *the* woman in Mick's life.[182]

In early 2002, Keith wrote a foreword to Robert Gordon's biography of Muddy Waters. Critics were surprised by his "rich, droll and crisply phrased prose style" (Sandford) and wondered whether they had got him wrong all along. When *Fortune* magazine called Mick "the sole business brain" behind the Stones, Keith observed, "We're a mom-and-pop operation. He's mom, I'm pop."[183]

Mick's *Goddess* album sold less than 1,000 copies in the UK on the day of its release, compared to the 95,000 copies of Robbie William's latest work. Keith said, "I think that everybody with the possible exception of Mick himself, has learned the lesson that he's really good when he's with the Stones. But when he ain't, I don't think anybody gives a fucking toss."[184]

On May 7, 2002, the Stones announced their 14th North American tour. The Stones met in Paris to record 4 new songs for their 40th anniversary hit

---

182 Ibid., 430.
183 Ibid., 431.
184 Ibid., 432.

compilation *Forty Licks*, the first release to combine their post–*Sticky Fingers* songs with the older material to which Klein's ABKO held the rights. When released on September 30, 2002, it went to number one in the United Kingdom and number 2 in the United States and made it to the top 10 in 29 other markets.[185]

This time the rehearsals in Toronto took six weeks. Prince Rupert, Michael Cohl, and many lawyers and accountants came and went. There were cover stories in everything from *The Economist* to *Vogue*. The Stones' entourage was bigger than ever before, including fashion advisers, hairdressers, personal trainers, and coaches. Their hotel room requirements lists became long and detailed. Mick was contractually entitled everywhere in the world to a wide-screen TV with a cricket channel, and there had to be a "medium white Casablanca lily arrangement with weeping eucalyptus" in his private exercise room.[186] A post on Keno's Gasland, one of the best fan sites, revealed many more details. Keith's room had to be entirely in black, and all alcohol had to be evacuated from Ronnie's minibar. Mick's wish list included two bottles of moderately priced red wine.

Mick's announcement to Keith on June 14, 2002 that he would be knighted almost brought the touring preparations to an end. Keith's reaction was unexpectedly violent. "I went beserk and bananas at [Jagger's] blind stupidity." Over time, he got used to the idea and called Mick "our lordship" or "His Royal Fucking Highness."[187]

On September 3, 2002, the Stones played the 1st of 117 *Licks* concerts in Boston. The tour spread over 23 countries in 5 legs and grossed $301,550,000 in the process. It was sponsored by the online stock-brokerage service E-Trade. The stage was the smallest in 30 years, with just a few props (a big screen and a B-stage). Artistically, the tour was fantastic, some say the best ever, and the Stones were pure electricity when on stage. They continued to vary their set list from venue to venue, including songs that had never been part of their stage repertoire. The venues included a mix of domes, arenas, and clubs. The Stones sold fewer tickets but at higher prices (up to $900 for the smaller venues). In Las Vegas, the hippy turned lawyer David Bonderman paid $7 million to have the Stones perform at his 60th birthday party. During the show, the tour entourage worked perfectly together, from technical and security crew to the personal assistants on standby who watched the slightest signals to bring out

---

185 Ibid., 434.
186 Ibid., 433.
187 Ibid., 430.

a drink or a cigarette. Many of the crew had served the Stones since the early 1970s. "By and large, the entourage was supremely competent, commendably loyal, fiercely partisan, and absolutely loathed one another. The single aide who had the Stones' collective and wholehearted backing, and knew it, was Rupert Loewenstein, who controlled the money."[188] In February 2003, the Stones played their first free concert since Altamont to support the Resources Defense Council, an environmental organization, and even the Chinese Government granted the Stones the permission to perform (except a few blacklisted songs such as "Brown Sugar" that contained "spiritual pollution"). However, the concerts were canceled because of the SARS panic. In February 2003, the Stones played their first concert in India, with ticket prices between $6 and $25. "We're happy to be here. Sorry we're about forty years late," Mick announced. In Germany, the Stones' yearlong security manager Jim Callahan was arrested by the police for privately reselling VIP passes at high prices; he was placed on indefinite leave of absence. On September 20, the Stones played at Twickenham Stadium. Charlie gave an interview to BBC's Charlie Gillett and afterward sent him a handwritten thank you note signed with his name and the words "Drummer for the Rolling Stones."[189] The *Forty Licks* tour formally ended on October 2 in Zurich, but one month later the Stones played for the first time on Chinese Soil (Hong Kong), opening with "Brown Sugar."

In June 2004, Keith and Mick met in France to work in Mick's home studio on *A Bigger Bang*, their first studio album since 1997, while Michael Cohl was working on the next tour. There they received a call from Shirley Watts; Charlie had throat cancer. Ronnie was in detox, again. For a moment, Mick and Keith thought about scrapping the plans but ultimately decided to go on. In parallel, Mick worked with the *Eurythmics'* Dave Stewart on the soundtrack for the remake of *Alfie*. Early in 2005, Mick and Keith took the tapes to Ocean Way Studios in Hollywood to have them polished by Don Was. Michael Cohl had lined up the mortgage company Ameriquest as tour sponsor. The tickets, priced between $75 and $450, sold out instantly. At that time, Ameriquest had to settle a lawsuit for some $325 million with the US government that had accused it of charging hidden fees to consumers. Media described the company as "ethically bankrupt," "voraciously aggressive," and "complete vultures."

---

188 Ibid., 437.
189 Ibid., 439.

When asked why the Stones worked with such a controversial sponsor, Mick replied, "They offered us the most money."[190]

On May 3, 2005, all band members passed their mandatory pre-tour physicals. It was during one of these physicals that Ronnie was found to exceed the permitted alcohol level by a factor of 17. His hotel requirements list specified that the minibar had to be emptied but for chocolate, juice, and mineral water. A week later, they announced their new tour on the stage of New York's Julliard School and played three songs, including the new "Oh No, Not You Again," an instant classic. *A Bigger Bang* was released on September 5, 2005. With its 16 songs and more than an hour of playing time, it was the 2nd longest album after *Exile*. There are some great songs, many interesting tracks, and only two or three weak ones. Prior to the album's release, Mick and Keith had argued about the inclusion of Mick's "Sweet Neo Con," a critical satire about the Iraq events and the neoconservatives. Mick insisted on having the song on the album. Keith's reluctance was not primarily driven by the fact that he lived in Connecticut. Also, he had supported Tony Blair's war efforts by a letter ("Stick to your guns, Tony").[191] Keith's main hesitation was that the Stones, as a matter of principle, wrote lyrics in metaphorical style. The album went to number two in the British charts and number three in the United States; it sold three million copies worldwide.

The *Biggest Bang* tour opened at Boston's Fenway Park on August 21, 2005. With its 200-ton stage structure, the Stones had gone back to their usual standards. By December 5, the tour had grossed $162 million, shattering the record set by the *Bridges* tour. Mick had sold a luxury box to Governor Arnold Schwarzenegger, which allowed the latter to invite supports in exchange for campaign contributions. Mick's statement that it was all about "four guys having fun" and "not giving a shot about the business side" may have been a slight exaggeration. The Stones, nevertheless, did enjoy performing together, and they continued to take risks by adding rarely played songs, and even songs by other artists, to their set list. For a concert in Austin, Texas, Keith would spend morning time in his hotel to rehearse "Learning the Game," a country song by Buddy Holly. For their performance at the Janet Jackson–traumatized Super Bowl in Detroit on February 5, 2006, the TV network turned down the microphone whenever Mick was approaching a questionable word. Two weeks later, the Stones played a free concert at Rio de Janeiro's Copacabana in front

---

190 Ibid., 441.
191 Ibid., 438.

of a crowd of 1.6 million. The *Biggest Bang* DVD set, unlike the 2021 rerelease, included not only the concert but a very interesting 45-minute documentary on the logistics required to prepare the concert over a period of two weeks. The mammoth show required over 500 lights, hundreds of speakers, and a video screen 13 meters long. The audience was spread over a beach area of 2.5 kilometers, which required the sound systems to use a relay pattern to keep the sound in sync; for every 350 meters the sound had to be delayed by an additional second.

In April 2006, the Stones finally played for the first time in mainland China. For their concert in Shanghai they replaced "Brown Sugar" by "Bitch." After a concert in New Zealand, the Stones retired to the Wakaya Club in Fiji for a few days of rest. It was there that Keith accidentally banged his head against a tree and had to undergo emergency surgery in Auckland, where he was flown to by air ambulance. The doctors prescribed six months of rest, and the tour had to be interrupted. The insurance company paid $14 million in lost receipts.

During the forced break, Keith had a short appearance in *Pirates of the Caribbean* as Johnny Depp's father, a movie produced by Disney. On the day of the movie's release, Keith told the press, in response to a question about his drug experiences, that he had once snorted the ashes of his deceased father after the urn he kept at home had accidentally broken.

After Keith's return to the stage, the Stones resumed their *Biggest Bang* tour with 40 shows in Europe and North America, after 10 days of rehearsals in a school gym in Vilvoorde, a small Flemish town outside Brussels in Belgium. The tour contract specified that Mick had to be absent from the stage during Keith's two-song mini set; Mick would go backstage and strap on his oxygen mask.

In August 2006, Keith and Charlie sat down with Prince Rupert and the Dutch accountant Johannes Flavie to create a pair of Amsterdam-based foundations that would allow them to pass on their assets to their heirs tax-free after their death.[192]

On October 29 and 30, 2006, the Stones performed two concerts at the 2,800-seat Beacon Theatre in New York, filmed by Martin Scorsese and a crew of 17 camera operators, including the Maysles Brothers who had shot the Altamont concert for *Gimme Shelter*. The concert movie *Shine a Light* is most entertaining, as it captures the musician's gestures and facial expressions as

---

192 Ibid., 447.

they evolve with the music, with an average cut every three to four seconds. The "making of" parts on the DVD reveal insights into the Stones' working methods, entourage, and their comical, self-derisional talent. Just before the first concert, at a birthday event for Bill Clinton, Ahmet Ertegun tripped over backstage, hit his head, and fell into a coma. He died six weeks later. After the second concert, Mick flew home to visit his father for a last time just before he died. A few months later, Keith would spend a night at his mother's deathbed, picking on his guitar.

Meanwhile, the Stones began the eighth and last leg of their tour, having already played in 32 countries over a period of 22 months. On June 10, 2007, they played at the Isle of Wight festival but declined to appear in Glastonbury after the festival organizers refused to pay the £1 million appearance fee. *Forbes* magazine placed the Stones at the top of the music moneymaking list. After two years, 147 shows and $560 million in gross revenues, the *Biggest Bang* tour closed with three concerts in London's O2 Arena. Each of the Stones earned some $45 million or £30 million. Critics were generally supportive about the Stones' performance, but voices expressed concern about Keith's ability to concentrate and play the guitar after his accident and developing arthritis.

With the tour being over, the Stones resumed their private lives and individual interests. Mick went back to film production, to the practice of Buddhism and daily meditation, and Keith retired to his Caribbean homes, supporting friends here and there with some guitar licks on their albums and posed for Louis Vuitton advertisements. He would soon start to write his tremendously successful autobiography *Life*. Charlie retreated to his farm in Devon to raise horses and sheepdogs, and Woody pursued his detox efforts and published his surprisingly honest autobiography *Ronnie*, in which he tells how naive he was in entrusting the management of his money to others until one day Prince Rupert sat at his hotel bedside saying, "Ronnie, you're not gonna make it." All denied rumors, if any, that the band had split.

In July 2008, Mick signed a new contract with Vivendi's Universal Music Group (UMG), which paid the Stones $15 million upfront and guaranteed $120 million over four years. The worldwide contract covered three new albums and the rights to release the post-1971 catalog for about five years. The contract brought the Rolling Stones' entire output under a single roof, since Universal had already distributed the band's pre-1971 music through the ABKCO label. This deal, however, did not include the publishing rights, which remained with EMI. UMG's first step to a return on investment was the issuing of the 2009 remasters of all post-Klein Stones studio albums. Fans and critics noticed that the 2009 re-masters were not noticeably better than the 1994 re-masters by Virgin.

That criticism is unjustified. The 2009 reissues had a much clearer sound and a higher level of musical detail. However, one could criticize that the sound was still somewhat compressed, lagging behind the work realized by some of the talented bootleggers such as the remastering of *Goats Head Soup* by the famous Mickboy.

Together with the 2009 re-masters, the Stones also issued a new edition of *Exile*, with a bonus CD that included 10 previously unreleased basic tracks that had been enriched by recently added lyrics, licks, and grooves. The reissue in May 2010 entered the number one position in the UK charts, a first for the reissue of a classic. A similar exercise was done with *Some Girls*. While the main album's music is quite edgy, the bonus CD includes mostly softer country rock songs, colored by accordions and marimbas with a touch of Hawaii sound, probably the Stones' truly preferred music. For commercial reasons, and to counter the punk movement, these softer songs had not made it onto the original album. In October 2010, the Stones released *Ladies and Gentlemen: The Rolling Stones*, a remastered and enriched documentary on their 1972 US tour that had been released originally in 1974 to theaters but never for home view. October 2011 saw the release of the concert CD/DVD "The Rolling Stones: Some Girls Live in Texas '78." The Stones also started to open their vaults by making available for download several legendary live recordings from the 1970s that had been available as unofficial bootlegs only. In the meantime, more vault content has been released as CD/DVD/Vinyl under the label *From the Vault*.

The year 2011 also saw another project in which Mick was involved, *SuperHeavy*, a one-off effort by Dave Stewart, Damian Marley, A. M. Rahman, Joss Stone, and Mick. It had an eclectic mix of different styles, from reggae to Indian, with Mick's characteristic timbre, and it was (and still is) extremely pleasant to listen to and a truly collective effort on its own.

5. 50 and Counting[193]

In 2012, the Stones started to celebrate their 50th anniversary. The band made a public appearance at the Marquee Club in London on July 12, 2012, the 50th anniversary of their first-ever concert. Fans hoping for a new studio album and a tour were disappointed. The Stones issued a coffee-table book titled *50* and

---

193 Thanks to Wikipedia for providing detailed information on the many events of this decade.

had the tongue logo redesigned by Shepard Fairey. He was likely paid more than his predecessor John Pasche.

October 2012 saw the release of a career-spanning documentary *Crossfire Hurricane*, directed by Brett Morgen, who had conducted some 50 hours of interviews with the Stones, including the "leavers" Bill Wyman and Mick Taylor.

In November 2012, the Stones released another compilation album, *Grrr!*, available as 2 CDs version, 3 CDs version, 4 CDs version, and a Deluxe version with 4 CDs, Vinyl LP, and booklet. It included only two new tracks, "Doom and Gloom" and "One More Shot," recorded at Studio Guillaume Tell in Paris during August 2012. Like *Forty Licks*, it covered the Decca and post-Decca years. The album went to number 3 in the UK and number 19 in the United States, and it sold 1.4 million copies.

On October 15, 2012, the band announced to the pleasure of their fans their first shows at the O2 Arena in London, the Barclays Center in Brooklyn, and at the Prudential Center in Newark, New Jersey. In October and November, the band conducted rehearsals in Bondy near Paris (in a rehearsal studio named Planet Live) and in the Wembley Arena in London. In the days preceding the Newark gig, the band met in a studio in Weehawken, New Jersey, for secretive, preliminary rehearsals. Mick Jagger performed in *Saturday Night Live*, where he would become a regular guest for a number of years. One of two Newark shows was broadcasted in pay-per-view in the United States and many other countries. Tour guests included Bill Wyman, Mick Taylor, Mary J. Blige, Jeff Beck, Eric Clapton, Florence Welch, Gary Clark Jr., John Mayer, Bruce Springsteen, Lady Gaga, and the Black Keys. The 2012 leg also included two secret shows in Paris in October; in December, the band participated in the Concert for Sandy Relief.

Later, more shows were added under the label "50 & Counting" tours. Between then and July 2013, the Stones would play some 30 concerts in a variety of cities in the United States, Canada, and Europe (London and Paris), with an avalanche of guest stars from Eric Clapton to Lady Gaga. The Stones also appeared—for the first time—at Glastonbury Festival in June 2013 and—for the second time—at Hyde Park in July 2013 (coinciding with Mick's 70th birthday). The Frankfurter Allgemeine Zeitung wrote about the Hyde Park concert: "All skepticism had disappeared after the first three minutes." A live CD/DVD "Sweet Summer Sun: Live in Hyde Park" was released in October 2013.

In June 2013, Mick and Keith, *not* the Rolling Stones, entered into a *publishing* (not distribution) deal with Bertelmann's music subsidiary, BMG. This deal has an interesting structure. First, Mick and Keith appointed BMG to take on, as of July 1, 2013, direct responsibility for publishing all songs written by Jagger/Richards since 1983. Second, BMG was charged with handling the Jagger/Richards shares of their pre-1983 copyrights, which are represented by ABKCO and EMI Music Publishing. Third, it covered all future work. The responsibilities of BMG range from marketing and licensing the songs to the film, TV, and advertising sectors and to ensuring that the writers are paid promptly and accurately for their use on the fast-growing number of digital music services. The BMG press release had been vague in terms of the deal scope, which compelled ABKCO to clarify that "in light of today's announcement … , ABKCO Music, Inc. wishes to reiterate that ABKCO, and ABKCO alone, owns and controls 100% of the worldwide copyright to the original 1963-1971 publishing catalogue of Jagger/Richards Rolling Stones compositions," that is, that it controls the copyrights.

In December 2013, the band announced the "14 on Fire" tour, a follow-up to the 50 & Counting tour, which was to visit the Middle East, Asia, Europe, and Australia. The tour was very similar to the 50 & Counting tour, as was the 1990 "Urban Jungle" portion of the *Steel Wheels* tour to the 1989 *Steel Wheels* portion. It had the same stage design, set list structure, and clothing/merchandise, and it had Mick Taylor as a guest. The tour included a first time show in Abu Dhabi, a one-off show at the Shanghai Mercedes-Benz Arena, a one-night only show at the Singapore Marina Bay Sands Grand Ballroom, the Pinkpop Festival in the Netherlands, the TW Classic Festival in Belgium, and two one-off shows in Germany. The tour had to be interrupted after the unexpected passing of L'Wren Scott. The Australia and New Zealand shows were postponed with new dates to be scheduled. The tour also included a first-ever appearance in Israel, dubbed by Haaretz as being "Historic with a capital H." In 1965, Prime Minister David Ben-Gurion had canceled a performance out of fear that rock music might corrupt the youth. A show at Hanging Rock in November was canceled due to Mick Jagger having a throat infection. On the last day of tour rehearsals, the band invited 27 fans to an intimate 11 song set.

The "Zip Code" tour began in May 2015 in San Diego and traveled across North America before concluding in July 2015 in Quebec City, Canada. The name is a reference to the artwork for *Sticky Fingers*, which had its entire track list played during the Zip Code tour. A live CD and a corresponding concert movie were released subsequently, as well as a deluxe rerelease of *Sticky Fingers* with abundant alternate takes (Eric Clapton on "Brown Sugar") and live material from 1970.

The "América Latina Olé" tour began on February 3, 2016, in Santiago and visited La Plata, Montevideo, Rio de Janeiro, São Paulo, Porto Alegre,

Lima, Bogotá, and Mexico City. It ended with a free concert in Havana on March 25, 2016, Good Friday. It would be the first open-air concert in the country by a British rock band at, but not inside, the Coliseo de la Ciudad Deportiva de La Habana. The concert was used for a live CD and concert movie *Havana Moon*, which differed from others by very extensively zooming in on the genuinely enthusiastic and grateful audience, from old to young, for all of whom this was a first-ever lifetime experience.

Later, the band released the 140-minutes-long tour documentary *Olé Olé*, covering the tour, with only a few scenes from concerts. The movie has several interesting narratives: (i) It highlights the passionate dedication of the Latin American fans for whom the Rolling Stones were not just music but sparks of light and freedom falling into the drop zones of poverty and political repression. (ii) It suggests that the Rolling Stones are more than a band: creators of a way of life in the tradition of the Pythagorean philosophical school where philosophy was taught not as abstract science but as a way of life and key to a happy life. (iii) Almost to counterbalance this observation, the Stones' members emphasize repeatedly that they did not bring this dedication about intentionally, and they use language reflecting their self-awareness of having "received" a gift that they were able to share with others. They do not expressly specify the source of that benediction. (iv) The documentary provides many details into the complicated logistics of a world tour, with two identical stage scenes being shipped around the globe for alternate use. Surprisingly many of the latter sequences deal with the ongoing planning of the Havana concert, which remained an uncertainty until a very late stage when the tour was already underway. (v) Each of the four band members reveals a key influence from his childhood years that signifies a career-spanning driver: painting for Ronnie (an activity where he is the boss), Grandpa Gus's guitar for Keith, accompanying other musicians for Charlie, and acting out impersonations in the family circle for Mick, forcing him to overcome his shyness. (vi) A carefully built-up subtext of the movie is the justification for playing the Havana concert on Good Friday, notwithstanding the unexpected and unsuccessful intervention of Pope Francis a few days before the concert. As different sequences through the documentary reveal from the outset, the concert was initially planned for March 20 but had to be postponed at the request of the Cuban Government due to the impromptu visit to Cuba by US president Obama. The movie suggests that Good Friday was the only available option resulting from a conjecture of the government's request and logistical challenges—the stage had to be flown in from Belgium. While the movie shows Keith commenting on the Pope's intervention sarcastically, Mick remains silent on this issue. Other parts of the documentary show Mick reflecting on his life in front of a picture of the Christ in a cemetery chapel, and the Cristo Redentor of Rio de Janeiro is also briefly shown (as in the earlier documentary of the Copacabana concert). In another part of the documentary, the origins of local music are stated to be "in reaction to the Catholic church"—all in all, a subtle mix of messages blending different spiritual viewpoints of Mick and Keith. Eventually, the Rolling Stones would release another post-Decca compilation "Honk" on April 19, 2019, another Good Friday.

On December 2, 2016, the Stones released *Blue & Lonesome*, an album with 12 blues covers, recorded in British Grove Studios in December 2015. The album reached number one in the UK, the second-highest opening sales week for an album that year. In July 2017, press reports announced that the band was about to record a new album of original material, for which fans are still waiting at the time this is written (fans can look forward to a new album being released in 2022 before, during or after the "Sixties" European tour). In December 2017, the Stones released *On Air*, a collection of BBC recordings from 1963 to 1965.

The year 2016 also saw the Stones entering the museum universe with "Exhibitionism," a nostalgic display of studios at London's Saatchi Gallery, guitars, equipment, and other items. Big fun for fans who are into memorabilia. A bit like the Freud Museum in Vienna, where you can see the original furniture of Freud's apartment and the hat he used to wear when he was not thinking. The exhibition would travel to several countries under the name "UNZIPPED." In April 2021, it resided in the Netherlands at the Groninger Museum; in July 2021, it had moved to TheMuseum in Kitchener, Southern Ontario, delivered by DHL. A recent check on the internet (January 2022) suggests that the exhibition is still there.

The "No Filter" Tour began in September 2017 in Hamburg and had to be interrupted due to the COVID-19 pandemic after the August 2019 gig in Miami Gardens, Florida. It would turn out to be Charlie's last show. With 28 shows in Europe and 17 in the United States, with an overall attendance of 1.5 million fans, and grossing $235 million, the tour was one of the most commercially successful concert tours of 2017 and 2018. The tour was briefly interrupted in March 2019 due to Mick Jagger's heart condition. All but one of the remaining shows were rescheduled, except the band's headline performance at the New Orleans Jazz Festival. The replacement act, Fleetwood Mac, also had to be canceled for health reasons, and both bands were ultimately replaced by Widespread Panic. The tour resumed but had to be canceled again due to COVID-19.

During the pandemic, the Stones participated from their respective homes in the "One World: Together at Home" project and released a single called

"Living in a Ghost Town," the material coming from the album project and the lyrics being adapted to the circumstances. A very successful reissue of *Goats Head Soup* included unreleased outtakes and a high-quality song featuring Jimmy Page ("Scarlet"); the Stones became the first band to top the chart across six different decades. Netflix produced an insightful documentary on Keith (*Under the Influence*), and Ronnie released an autobiographic documentary called *Somebody Up There Likes Me*. Finally, Mick starred in another movie (*Burnt Orange Heresy*). Critics say that even he could not save the movie from its weak plot.

Brussels Affairs, one of the most famous bootlegs due to the great set list of the 1973 tour, the fabulous horn section, and the relentless energy of the band, was officially released as part of *From the Vault* in Japan a few years ago and in the rest of the world as part of the *Goats Head Soup* reissue in 2020. At the very end of their 1973 tour, the band played two shows in Brussels' Forest venue. "What's interesting about these bootlegs is the band don't know they're being recorded, so they don't give a shit, and they're playing what they're playing and you get a natural feel, you know?" (Keith).

In September 2020, the Stones opened their first permanent merchandising boutique in Carnaby Street in London's West End, where fans can buy Stones-themed crystal decanters made by Baccarat (£535), Stones red bomber jackets (£110), a rubberized raincoat made by Stutterheim (£235), or face masks made from cotton or silk. The Carnaby store is run in partnership with the merchandising company Bravado. Last but not least, and very importantly, John Pasche got his second chance: the store sells some of his limited edition artworks for £1,195. Says David Boyne, managing director of Bravado, "They remain really relevant but I don't think you can escape the rich history they have too. They have an amazing past but a really exciting present and future."[194]

In December 2020, the 2013 publishing deal with BMG was extended to include neighboring rights, only six months after BMG's launch of its neighboring rights service offering.

In early 2021, Mick released a song coproduced with Dave Grohl of the Foo Fighters, "Easy Sleazy." In the tradition of "England Lost" but much more angry and dynamic, it is another social comment type of song performed in the attitude of a scornful biblical prophet.

---

194 Mark Brown, *The Guardian* (September 8, 2020).

In July 2021, news was that the Stones rescheduled concerts in the United States, thereby continuing their interrupted No Filter tour.

Charlie's withdrawal from the tour for medical reasons in early August was the first reminder that the Stones members are now close to 80 years old. Having Steve Jordan sit in for Charlie was not a shock to fans. He has been a friend of the Stones for many decades and is Keith's artistic partner in his solo efforts. Steve was reportedly designated by Charlie himself. We owe Steve the wonderful "Almost Hear You Sigh." This being said, the fan community— and probably everyone outside the Watts family—was surprised when media announced Charlie's death on August 24. Outsiders may have thought that Charlie had a medical issue and would possibly never return on stage, but nobody outside the inner circle expected his imminent passing. Was Charlie aware of his state when commenting with his usually subtle humor: "For once my *timing* has been a little *off*"?

Posts from the No Filter tour on social media revealed how much the discreet Charlie had been crucial for the band and the backbone for the more extroverted joyful stage action of his fellow band members for all these years. As great as the No Filter concerts were, the bold self-confidence of the Stones seemed somewhat diminished. It was as if the surviving Stones were shell-shocked. They probably were. During the first concert without Charlie, the great Mick appeared to be on the verge of shedding a tear, saying, "I'm losing it." In between concerts, fans and journalists could spot Mick on the balcony of his Miami hotel displaying a grumpy mood and wearing phototherapy glasses.

A last innovative feature to be mentioned is Mick's and Ronnie's particularly active use of social media, notably Instagram, that emerged in 2021 and continues ahead of the "Sixties" European tour. These frequently humorous posts reach an unprecedented level of intimacy and signal that the world, despite everything that is currently going on in Europe, still has some joyful and meaningful events to look forward to this spring 2022.

As this book goes to print, the Stones are gearing up for their "Sixties" European tour. I purchased a few tickets for myself and a few selected clients, and I was surprised to realize how much I look forward to the event, both musically and emotionally. FT's Claer Barrett reports that the Stones set up a financial literacy training programme for their roadies, teaching them financial planning in the gig economy.[195] Moreover Keith "leaked" that a new album

---

195 "What the Rolling Stones roadies can teach you about money", FT of April 12, 2022, https://www.ft.com/content/80642963-f978-4868-a1b5-e7769b80cc3b.

with new songs will be released this year, with Steve Jordan playing some of the drums part. It is amazing to see how naturally Steve, the successor designated by Charlie, blends with the band in terms of style and sound. First short video clips showing Mick perform an unknown song ("Really Wanna Tell the Truth?") let us expect another masterpiece full of music, wisdom and wit.

We cross fingers that more will hopefully follow. Amen.

C. SOME VIRTUES (OUTRO)

What a life!

Rocking on stage at age 80 and having millions of fans rejoice and pay for it, that is what a dream life looks like. Having amassed personal fortunes sizable enough to feed generations of descendants and living a comfortable life, enjoying the pleasures of being surrounded by offspring while still catching media attention with every word uttered, there are not many people on this planet at a similar level.

In addition to the material wealth, the Stones can look back on their great musical legacy. There will always be several categories of Stones worshippers: those who love the band's attitude and image, those who enjoy mostly their great hits from "Satisfaction" to "Start Me Up," and those who are deeply into their groove. For a good reason, as the Stones have created a musical language of their own that makes it fascinating to listen to and figure out the texture of any Stones song. The way Charlie hits his cymbals; the multiform licks of Ronnie and Keith; the expressive bandwidth of Mick's voice, from scornful to lustful, arrogant, sensual, and melancholic; and the dramaturgy of the songs, fans just love it without ever getting tired of it. And this even though none of them is at their best when alone. Only together do they reach their full potential.

This phenomenal artistic and financial success did not fall from the sky. It required vision, hard work, and discipline, kept up faultlessly over six decades now. For each of them, the success has come at a price. When Mick and Keith connected for the first time, they would not know that their whole lives would become so intimately intertwined. And that is difficult. Centuries ago, young boys would enter the monastery to keep up a strict religious discipline until their death. What the Stones went through is not that dissimilar. And for those like Charlie, the loyal keeper of the beat, it meant waiting, waiting, and more waiting. To be on tour for six months, twelve months, or two years, with concerts every other day—who can imagine the courage it must require to go on stage over and over again, including on the headache days when morale is down for personal reasons? And to overcome all these inevitable interpersonal tensions? Ultimately, the question any Stones member had to ask themselves was, "Is it worth taking all this shit?" For Bill and Mick T. it was not. For Charlie and Stu it was.

It also seems clear that even the late Stones are not just about the money. As Keith said it, getting on stage in filled stadiums is good for "ego gratification." Their desire to perform music, to invent new music, and to express themselves musically has never faded. The passion has been there all the time, and this is what fans appreciate, even if they don't know the new songs as well as the old. The past of the Stones attracts us because there is still a present after 60 years, with hope for a future.

Whoever starts a business today is statistically unlikely to make it last 60 years, as things evolve so rapidly now. But then, you never know when you start. But if you have a good start with a positive outlook for the future, you may learn some lessons from the Stones' story of success.

The Rolling Stones are a collective business venture from the outset. They are not just the idea of one brilliant individual. Several people started the project together, and the miracle was to succeed in turning this multi-personal project into what it is today. The secret of success is to have maintained the buy-in of most band members for 45 (Ronnie) to 60 years now (Mick, Keith, and the late Charlie). This is the result of a complex, subtle, and ultimately successful balancing of complementary personalities with complementary skill sets and diverging personal and professional aspirations. It is the result of finding a way of bearing with each other's deficiencies and developing mutual respect. The ability to forgive each other is an essential part of the story.

Every long-term success has a few ingredients that are identifiable at least in hindsight. Below are a few, there may be many others:

Project

The first essential requirement is to have a project. The Stones started out with the project to cater Afro-American blues to a white audience in London. Certainly, money, sex, and fame may have been on their minds. Who does not dream to be Lancelot? However, had they been driven primarily by commercial considerations, they would have played a style of music that was fashionable in the early 1960s, which they did not. Thus, there project must have been rooted in a genuine passion, and all Stones have confirmed this at one point or another. It was a sign of genuine passion to sit in an unheated apartment and listen to blues records over and over again until all notes are fully figured out. And they were figured out, as everyone who listens to the blues originals can tell. It was a lucky coincidence that all original Stones members shared the same passion, albeit in different declinations. Brian was the pure blues purist who had never heard about Chuck Berry before he met Keith. Keith liked both blues and Chuck Berry, but he did not like pop. Mick, on the other hand, liked blues, Chuck Berry, but also liked to occasionally deviate into some pop or Elizabethan folklore. There was enough room to bridge the gaps and reconcile these nuances. It also allowed them to experiment with different styles in a view of catching an evolving audience and the Zeitgeist. Otherwise, they would have remained, in Stu's words, a "bloody Status Quo." Or they would have disappeared after a few years.

Talent

The second most essential requirement is to have talent. Not any talent but the talent required for the project in question. One can be a talented footballer, but that does not make them a violinist. Anyone who played in the Stones had a certain talent, but at different degrees. None of them was a virtuoso strictly speaking. Mick is not Caruso; Keith, Brian, and Ronnie are not Steve Vai. Bill is not Jaco Pastorius, and the late Charlie was not Billy Cobham. Mick T. came closest to being a virtuoso, but in the early 1970s, when speed was everything, he lost out to Ritchie Blackmore, John McLaughlin, Steve Van Halen, and even Jimmy Page. Then, being a virtuoso is not the most important talent a rock band must have, unless its project consists of being the fastest band on the planet. More importantly, there is no necessity to define virtuosity through speed. In classical music, a virtuoso is someone who masters his instrument phenomenally. Paganini was a violin virtuoso, and those who can play his music are virtuoso too. But no one listens to Paganini all the time. Once the initial astonishment is digested, it is very boring. Similarly, when rock grew out of its Kinderschuhe, supergroups like Cream, Ten Years After, Mahavishnu Orchestra, Deep Purple or Led Zeppelin played these technically complex, usually fast grooves with endless soli, most of which are no longer of interest today. It just happened that the Stones had exactly the talent that was required to be a blues and rock band. Maybe it evolved fueled by passion. The Stones played their instruments reasonably well; they had the ability to learn how to play the songs of their masters; and they were able to transcend their forerunners to create their own musical language. Therefore, some of the criticism that

could be read even in recent years is beside the point. In one review of *Blue &
Lonesome*, one could read that the Stones brought in Eric Clapton for two songs
because they were not good enough to play the guitar solos themselves. That
is nonsense. If the Stones called on their longtime friend Eric, it was because
they wanted to have his personal touch on their album. It is true that Eric plays
technically "better" (in the sense of "faster" and more developed solos) than
Ron and Keith, but if that were the test for inviting a guest, Ron and Keith
would never play on their own albums. Eric, just like Keith and Ron, has an
immediately recognizable signature, just as George Harrison had, and it must
have been a pleasure for the Stones to have an old friend add a nuance to their
album. Similarly, in another review of a 1999 tribute album for Jimmy Rogers
to which Mick and Keith contributed (together!), a critic wrote that Mick's
voice did not equal that of his blues fathers. Of course, it did not. Each voice
is unique. And it is not that all bluesmen were technically powerful baritones.
And they had very different voices. Thus, what matters is whether a band, with
its own specific means, can craft something that is worth to be listened to and
capable to hook the listeners up on a long-term basis. If that is the description
for talent, the Stones were talented. However, not every band member had the
talent to remain a member for a very long period of time. Brian was the first to
lose it, largely due to his psychological disposition with its touch of paranoia.
And maybe he did just not have the talent required to evolve with a band that
reached unexpected levels of success, which in turn required a different and
more sophisticated approach if the band were to continue. Mick T. also lacked
this ability but for different reasons. According to certain sources, the main
reason for his resignation was that he could no longer keep up with the level
of cocaine consumption that came with the tour live of the early 1970s. By the
time he left, his nasal bone had entirely disappeared. It must have been very
difficult to resist the different types of temptation in the Rolling Stones touring environment, and not everyone has Mick's iron discipline and self-control.
Mick T.'s frustration about the crediting policy may also have played a role, but
it was probably a rather secondary factor. Again, where a band shares a villa
to record an album over a period of six months, it is normal that a guitarist
comes up from time to time with a good riff that ends up structuring a song.
And maybe he should have been credited for this. But it is also conceivable
that as a matter of Glimmer Twins policy, such credits were kept to the usual
songwriters, if only for financial reasons. If crediting was essential for Mick T.
for financial reasons, could he not have asked for a simple increase? Bill, who
left after 30 years with the band, had the talent to stay with it another 30 years.
He elected not to. The Stones, mostly through Mick and Keith, also had the

talent to write more than 200 published songs, plus many more that remain unfinished in the vaults. Not every song is a masterpiece. Probably, 25 percent of the songs are masterpieces in the "Brown Sugar" league. Some 70 percent of the songs are in the range of "simply great music," and there are only a handful of songs that are badly built or otherwise unconvincing (and even this is a question of taste). That is a pretty good track record, due to the Stones' collective playing style, which gives the sound a texture that makes anything they play interesting, including simple jams during warm-ups and rehearsals.

Passion

The third most essential requirement is to have passion, and it better be genuine. The Stones started with the passion for blues, and this passion never left them. While they navigated and experimented over their long career, not only to stay in tune with changing times but also out of professional and artistic curiosity, they never abandoned their initial passion for the blues. Many blues-rock songs popped up on the bonus CDs that accompany the anniversary releases of original Stones albums. Others popped up earlier on strange compilation albums such as *Rarities* (released in 2005 and covering the 1971–2003 period). In the bonus part of *Shine a Light*, Keith is introvertedly picking his acoustic guitar while Mick and Ron are enthusiastically shaking hands with the Clintons. In 2016, the Stones released a full album of blues covers (*Blue & Lonesome*), and on YouTube there are clips where Keith and Ronnie are strumming their acoustic guitars accompanied by Mick's harmonica. Passion is the flame that fuels mind and body and which connects people through empathy. When interviewing young professionals for their first job, talent managers look at the hobbies listed at the end of the candidates' CVs and talk about these. An interview is not an oral examination; the candidates have no experience anyway, but they had an entire decade of teenage years to develop a passion, be it for reading, music, or playing in the soccer team.

Complementarity

Whenever a group of individuals starts a venture together, complementarity helps. First, complementarity at the level of skill set. That is the easiest part. Few bands hire more than one drummer. Second, outward-facing complementarity. Meaning that the audience must like what they see: diverse and differentiated individuals who interlock perfectly well. Alexandre Dumas's *Three Musketeers* (who in reality are four) are an early example of this type of complementarity:

one is the leader, another one is the reasonable guy, and the third one is funny. He has the most dangerous role. The Stones early on displayed a great complementarity of characters that people could identify with: Mick the diva, Keith the rebel, Mick T. the angel, Woody the clown, Charlie the gentleman, and Bill the bored bassist in the corner "fattening up the music." Third, complementarity has an inward side, which is the most important. To work together, people must like each other. To work together for 60 years requires the ability to not kill each other. In the world of submarines with missions of up to three months under the waterline without sun and fresh air, where the crew is compressed in a small space with no privacy, crew members do not speak to each other during the last two weeks on the way back home, as each word could be one word too many. The Stones always had that complementarity in all their lineups, although it was not always lasting, as in the case of Brian and Mick T. Mick and Keith were interdependent when it came to songwriting; Keith admired Mick's social ease; and Mick admired Keith's ability to play an instrument. While Mick played the harmonica very well from early on, it was only gradually that he picked up the guitar. In the 1970s, Mick would begin playing a guitar (or at least holding one) on stage, presumably to have a moment of physical rest where he could stop his hooting and hollering and prancing around. But this may also have been out of the desire to demonstrate his ability to play an instrument. There is even one slightly awkward moment: during the 1981 tour Mick grabbed a guitar as of the second song ("When the Whip Comes Down"), that is, too early to serve for rest, strums it with fast visible movements of his right hand, but the guitar is inaudible in the mix. Was it all for the vanity or had Keith ordered to shut the channel down? Keith and Mick T. were complementary in that one played lead, the other rhythm. It was the best use the Stones could make of Mick T.'s skill set, but it killed the two-guitar doctrine. Keith and Ronnie are complementary in that Ronnie is gifted with a particular kind of positive energy which he brings to the table every time the band gets together. He has a relaxing effect on Keith, while Mick T. did not. Charlie and Bill were complementary as the leading rhythm section in rock history, and Charlie was complementary with everyone in the band, a bit like the senior partner in a law firm. Finally, Ronnie was complementary to Mick and Keith, brokering peace in between them when things got more and more out of hand. Many short-lived acts lacked this inward complementarity, in particular, the so-called supergroups, where everyone wanted to shine as a star. Cream was an example for this. They started in 1966 and stopped in 1968, despite the top instrumentalists who composed the band. On their farewell live recording, *Goodbye*, two minutes of beautiful singing are the pretext for seven minutes of endless solos ("I'm So Glad"). Other groups simply failed because there were difficult personalities like Ritchie Blackmore or Jeff Beck.

Helping Hands

Our lives are not only what we do and eat but also whom we meet. In their launch phase, the Stones found helping hands—today they would be called business angels—who gave them the opportunity to present themselves. Alexis Korner and Giorgio Gomelsky are examples. Giorgio is particularly worth mentioning as he is probably the one who got least out of helping the Stones. Throughout their career, the Stones tried to help others as they had been helped. Examples include (but are not limited to) Marianne Faithfull, Anita Pallenberg, Tina Turner, Ronnie Lane, and many of the peers invited on stage for a song or two, from the old blues masters (Muddy Waters, Buddy Guy, Solomon Burke, and Taj Mahal) to young upcoming acts (Dave Matthews, Joss Stone, Justin Timberlake, Sheryl Crow, and many others). At a more advanced career level, the helping hands take the form of insourcing. From early on, the Stones called on additional musicians to enrich their sound. The first was the pianist Jack Nitzsche (not related to the philosopher). Nitzsche played with the Stones between 1965 and 1967 and introduced them to Ry Cooder, who would be a major influence on Keith, teaching him open tuning. The second was Nicky Hopkins, who would accompany the Stones until his premature death in 1994. He played on all studio albums of the Stones from *Between the Buttons* (1967) to *Tattoo You* (1981, except on *Some Girls*) and joined the Stones on several tours between 1971 and 1973. He could not make it to the 1973 European tour due to ill-health and never again joined the Stones' touring lineup. Billy Preston was called in on several occasions for his organ sound, until he blew the relationship by not following the rules. In a recent interview, Chuck Leavell, a former Allman Brother, spoke about his 40 years as "musical navigator" with and for the Stones.[1] Bobby Keys played saxophone on Stones albums from *Let It Bleed* (1969) to *Sweet Summer Sun* (2014); he died in the same year. Lisa Fischer and Bernard Fowler contributed soulful backup vocals to the Stones for many years. Sonny Rollins, Sugar Blue, and Flaco Jiménez contributed to several songs. The Stones also sourced in their various managers, and notably Prince Rupert (1968), the architect of their financial wealth, and they had recourse

---

1 https://www.businessinsider.com/the-rolling-stones-keyboardist-chuck-leavell-life-on-tour-2021-12?r=US&IR=T.

to trademark designers (John Pasche), stage equipment designers, and many more. For the big post-resurrection tours, a core group of up to 400 short-term employees collaborates with local suppliers in the different venues.

Sex Appeal

As strange as it may seem in our days, the Stones had sex appeal from day one, which contributed heavily to their success. Even as elder statesmen close to the eighth decade of their lifetime, they are still "sexy." In the beginning, it was mostly Mick who excited the younger audience members by his way of singing and moving (disgruntled early critics spoke of "repulsive sexual gymnastics"), and Brian cheered up the girls by his way of shaking his thick golden Nibelungen helmet hair. In the very early period Keith still looked like a reincarnation of Huckleberry Finn, but that changed quickly (e.g., on the cover album of *Out of Our Heads*), and the others also caught up. From around 1966 an impressive iconographic sophistication was in place thanks to numerous talented photographers who relentlessly took their pictures, and the pleasure of looking at Stones pictures never ceased. Fast-forwarding 20 years, their outrageous stage dress in flashy colors and intentionally bad taste was all part of a strategy that either was carefully designed or simply fell in place. Selling is seducing. The iconography operated as a visual pheromone that attracted fans and kept them stuck ("The Spider and the Fly") until the sweet venom of their music found its way through the ears into the brains to remain there for life. This gift was not given to the fabulous Herman and the Hermits despite exciting songs like "No Milk Today" or "My Reservation's Been Confirmed." In that respect, the Stones resemble makers of telecommunications devices that most people buy because of their appealing design and that just happen to be technically great at the same time.

Control

There are two types of control: control of the self and control of others. They frequently go in hand. Mick is the perfect control freak. Jean-Marie Périer, the French photographer associated with the magazine *Salut les copains* who traveled with the Stones during their first decade and took many great pictures of them on and off tours, wrote that Mick becomes a totally normal person the second he leaves the stage. Educated by a father who taught physical education in prestigious schools, Mick was used to physical discipline from early on. The way he looks and moves at age 78 is the proof of it. Whatever he consumed, he did so moderately. Mick coined the phrase about Tom Waits: "You should only let yourself go when you can bring yourself back." Bill is not known for control issues over food, drinks, or drugs. He smoked many cigarettes (visible in concert movies), probably to express his unbearable boredom while laying down the greatest bass lines in the history of mankind. Ronnie and Keith are known to have struggled with control issues for long periods of time, and they both managed to stop short of killing themselves and the band. Charlie, a family man who disliked being on long tours, struggled only at one point in his life. It may be that a drummer is better trained at being in control of himself, while guitarists can occasionally enjoy a bit of interpretative freedom. Control is also control of others, particularly those who take care of financials. In many professional services firms, the CFO is the single most important person. A CFO is what the Stones did not have before they met Prince Rupert. Andrew tried to push them into his secret agenda as hit producers for the Andrew Oldham Orchestra, unsuccessfully, and when the Stones decided to get rid of him, they did so very effectively. Easton and Klein were in a different league. Allen won their trust by obtaining large cash advances from Decca, but he failed to tell them that they should build up tax reserves. He also failed to mention that he registered the US publishing company under his name, and he managed to walk away with the entire song catalog of the first decade (1963–1969). After this painful experience, Mick swore to control everything. Even in the post-resurrection period when the Stones would sell their entire tours to industrial sponsors, no one could sell a single cup of beer in a concert venue without Mick having approved the vendor, the design of the cup, and the price of the beer. The Stones were far from being alone in trusting unreliable managers. The whole first generation of rock stars was financially illiterate, and even the well-established Stones had difficulties in finding a skilled person from an established firm to take charge of their business. Prince Rupert decided to leave his conservative merchant firm because in those days the rock scene was suspiciously frowned upon by good and ordinary citizens.

Determination

Not only is running a business a pleasure, but it also forces the leaders to take difficult decisions. The first such difficult decision was to eject Ian Stewart from the lineup, while keeping him on board for the rest of his prematurely ended life. It was in fact Andrew's decision; managers were powerful these days. The second was to get rid of Andrew. The third, and more difficult than the others, was to deal with Brian. Kicking out Klein was not a difficult decision; it was an easy decision which was difficult to carry out. The separation with Prince Rupert may have been difficult to decide, although it ended up as a rather amicable parting. Sixty years of rocking and rolling bring about many situations that need to be addressed, and some are mentioned above. Touring with a keyboardist who first refuses to leave the stage and then claims royalties on the live album must have been a difficult experience to deal with, even more as this was unexpected. The issue was solved by giving subsequent keyboarders fixed fee contracts to avoid repetition. Another type of determination is the imposition of leadership. The Stones had never been an Athenian democracy but rather an authoritarian regime. However, when Mick went ahead without consulting the band members about the acquisition of expensive stage equipment, that was constitutionally borderline. Commercially, it was one of the best decisions he may have taken. Those who attended the 1981–1982 tour, or any early post-resurrection concerts, remember how awe-inspiring the giant stage equipment with its many props and fireworks was, with Mick jogging miles while singing perfectly well into his mike.

Neutrality

Political and religious neutrality are well-known concepts. In many Western countries, members of the armed forces or the public administration are expected to observe political and religious neutrality, meaning that they should not display their affiliations ostensibly when exercising their public function. In professional services firms they are equally important, both for the well-being of the work force and in respect of a frequently diverse clientele. Most companies accommodate the exercise of faith requirements such as prayers or the observation of holidays within reasonable boundaries but ask firm members not to take public positions on political, religious, or societal issues where such position could be imputed to or negatively the firm. When the bailiff knocks at the door, who wants him to wear a T-shirt with a big "I love Jesus" or "Marx lives" printed across the chest? Neither should a judge display his political affiliation in the court room. In fact, in some professions a certain dress code is part of the game. Doctors are expected to wear white gowns, and few people would react with enthusiasm if their gastric surgeon displayed a mohawk on his head tattooed all around. The question of neutrality is also raised at the level of the company itself. It is a delicate question to be decided by each company whether it wants to take position on such issues, or on societal issues, and on which one. In popular music, some scenes are inherently political, such as the folk scene in the United States. However, artists of all kinds increasingly tend to take positions on issues such as freedom, democracy, the refugee crisis, gender, identity, peace, or the environment. In Cold War Germany in the late 1970s, pop acts supported antinuclear and anti-armament demonstrations mainly because their younger audience supported those. Frequently, the artists involved happened to be in a low of their artistic career. The Stones always had a policy of strict neutrality. Even "Street Fighting Man" was not a political song. A first important exception to the rule was one of the two studio tracks on the live album *Flashpoint* ("Highwire," 1991). A reaction to the first Gulf War, it criticized arms trading. The second important exception was "Sweet Neo Con" on *Bigger Bang* (2005), which criticized sarcastically the Cheney/Rumsfeld administration who had started the second Iraq War. This song led to intense debates between Mick and Keith. For Mick it was important to publish the critical song, and Keith, who lives in Connecticut, objected that as a matter of principal, the Stones only expressed themselves metaphorically. Other than that, the Stones supported several charity events dedicated to combat famine or commemorate terrorist acts and natural disasters. They do not seem to have taken position openly on other political, religious, or social issues. A similar neutrality applies to the charitable activities of the Stones. A percentage of tour profit goes to charitable causes, but the beneficiaries and the amounts are not published.

Business Acumen

To have good business acumen is helpful for anyone engaged in a business. The Stones set out on a long career path playing the blues, and their first album is 100 percent blues. The subsequent albums are more diverse, with a mix of blues, R&B, and pop rock but still aligned on the policy to focus on Afro-American music. Aftermath, the first album with own material, is more neurotic and white than Afro-American, but setting a trend. The two subsequent albums *Between the Buttons* and *Their Satanic Majesties Requests* are fully psychedelic but merely followed a trend. Did the Stones engage in this direction to enjoy musical diversification? The fact is that when listening to the early years, the quality of the material from that period is excellent and has aged well.[2] But

---

2 My preferred way of listening to the early material is to go to the "1963–1971" Collection on my streaming service, and then push the "shuffle" button. The early albums are not as conceptual as the later albums, and the random play emphasizes the beauty of the individual songs.

why did they abruptly go back to their original blues-rock approach? Their second psychedelic, self-produced album had earned harsh criticism notably on the production aspects (justified if compared to the Beatles' "Sgt. Pepper's"), but the psychedelic period was not yet over. The Stones could have hired a producer for another psychedelic album. They did not. It seems that the reconversion was self-determined, not following a trend. When the Stones released "Jumping Jack Flash," the results proved them right immediately. This time they were trendsetting. A similar intuition played a role when the Stones conceived their innovative 1972 US tour. Although the setlist was not much different from the 1969 US tour, the concept "intellectualized" the event, building up cultural credibility and social relevance. It is not clear whether this followed or set a trend, but it turned out to be the right thing. Follow-on innovation is also innovation: just as the switch from glam rock to edgy rock with *Some Girls* (1978) to counter the emergence of punk. The album was a commercial success. The bonus CD released with the 30th anniversary reissue contained mostly softer material, suggesting that the Stones hardened their style only to respond to a new trend. Again, they had done well. On two later albums (*Emotional Rescue*, 1980, and *Undercover*, 1983), fights took place between Mick and Keith over traditionalism (Keith) versus experimentation (Mick). Mick managed to place an experimental piece on each of the two albums (*Emotional Rescue* and *Too Much Blood*), and in both cases the songs contributed to giving the Stones a modern touch. The best business decision of the later years was to accept the proposal made by Michael Cohl to totally innovate the model of touring. It created a significant proportion of the Stones' overall wealth. Business acumen goes along with the ability to read the Zeitgeist, to self-question, adapt, and innovate (regardless of whether innovation is first or follow-on).

Luck

The Stones themselves say it with great humility. Their career could have been very different and much shorter, as there were many occasions on which things could have played out differently—a wrong artistic decision, a bad concert performance, etc. A subject rarely talked about is the physical security of the band members and their protection against physical assaults. Much of the "fuzz" around the Stones when appearing in public, for example, strongly built bodyguards pushing the Stones into black limousines looks like hyping it up. However, behind all of this hangs the lesson learned from John Lennon's assassination in the daytime streets of New York. When the Stones played in indoor venues or in stadiums in the pre-drone era, these venues could be easily secured. However, in the video documentary of the Copacabana concert, the nervousness is palpable when Cohl tells Mick about the 1.5 million people gathering on the beach longed by hotels with high rooftops. Luckily, very few individuals are exposed to that level of risk.

The Four "F"

Fairness, Fidelity, Forgiveness, Faith. If there is a credo for "working together," it can be summarized in these four Fs. *Fairness* relates to the way in which band members and external suppliers are treated and remunerated. Fairness does not mean communism. In the Stones, the songwriting duo earns most and keeps tight control over the credit allocation policy. But tour revenues are shared in equal parts with equity members. Other original band members such as Bill and Charlie were paid well, in particular, Charlie, who lived through the post-resurrection phase with its big touring revenues. However, Bill once stated that he left as soon as he had the necessary change to finance his lifestyle, that is, he was okay money-wise at the time of his departure. Ronnie had to wait a long time before making equity, and although he was not eligible for Promogroup financial management services in 2006, he had by then acquired the modest sum of £70 million. The arrangements with Darryl Jones are not known, but he is said to have $8 million in the bank, presumably mostly from his work with the Stones. In the earlier band days, one-off suppliers like John Pasche were paid very little, although their payment was still market standard (otherwise they would not have accepted the job). *Fidelity* means that individuals are properly valued. The Stones think long term. Most of their current touring family has been with them for 30 to 40 years, and the late Bobby Keys played with them for 45 years. He was non grata for several years due to a tour incident but made it back thanks to Keith. Nevertheless, if the working experience is good, the Stones keep their touring family together. Anita and Marianne remained on the payroll long after the end of their affiliation with Mick and Keith. Lisa Fischer traveled with the Stones between 1989 and 2014. She retired to pursue her solo career. Like Bernard Fowler, Lisa has manifold interests far beyond rock music that she can pursue with the support of the money earned with the Stones. She is credited with a net worth of $18. *Forgiveness* is an essential factor in any long-term relationship, professional or private. Nobody is perfect, and people hurt others intentionally and unintentionally all the time. A warm greeting ("You look well today") can be misunderstood based on distorted perception ("Didn't I look good the other days?"). A working relationship requires the ability to forgive—it also requires the ability to accept forgiveness by others. Politicians are well-trained in that task due to their constantly shifting alliances. In a rock band, people also get hurt. Bill and Mick T. felt hurt. Rightly or wrongly, they felt underappreciated and not respected. Mick and Keith hurt each other all the time. It is obvious that many of Mick's actions did hurt Keith. Again, it does not matter whether Keith's feeling was objectively justified or not. All that matters is that the feeling was real. It is less clear whether Mick felt hurt by Keith's nasty comments. If so, he would not have shown it. When Mick unleashed a war by releasing his first solo album in 1985, with Keith firing all his guns, Mick gave an interview wearing heavy makeup, resembling an upset women protesting her husband's conjugal violence over TV. Anyway, all that matters is that they both made it. They may not have transformed their complicated relationship of 60 years, but they manage to manage it and they are happy that they did. This result was made possible by faith: *Faith* (submission to higher authority) not meaning a confessional belief. It means that all band members concerned came to believe that they were part of something bigger, that they had received a gift they had to pass on to others: a gift that also led them to behave more responsibly. The Stones are today a family organization: not just a family but an organization for families. From grandma to toddler, the Stones have become a model of reference beyond their musical legacy.

The 10 Commandments of Working Together

If there were "10 commandments" by the Rolling Stones for successful working together, they could read like this:

The 10 Commandments for Working Together

First Commandment
Have a shared vision of doing something great, fueled by a collective passion.

Second Commandment
Be and remain collectively creative, perseverant, disciplined, agile, and adaptive; have courage to make changes.

Third Commandment
Encourage the emergence of an accepted consensual leadership structure. It helps.

Fourth Commandment
Respect your partners and value their respective contributions; support them in being successful contributors.

Fifth Commandment
Consider the individual aspirations of your partners if backed up by talent and aligned with the firm's overall strategy.

Sixth Commandment
Ensure a fair distribution of profits; combine equal base shares with flexible rewards for different contributions.

Seventh Commandment
Bear with each other and control your jealousy. Don't be vindictive; forgive each other, again and again.

Eighth Commandment
Aim at continuity, and avoid wasting your people. They help you succeed.

Ninth Commandment
Limit expulsions to counter genuine business threats, not internal power challenges.

Tenth Commandment
Never forget that "this is bigger than us." That includes the front man.

D. DRAMATIS PERSONAE (IN ORDER OF APPEARANCE)[1]

Alexis Korner

Alexis Andrew Nicholas Koerner was born in Paris in 1928. His father was an Austrian Jew, and his mother was half-Turkish and half-Greek. After a childhood in France, Switzerland, and North Africa his family moved to London, England, in 1940. A key souvenir was he listening to a record by the black blues pianist Jimmy Yancey during an air raid. "From then on all I wanted to do was play the blues." After the war, Korner played piano and guitar and joined Chris Barber's Jazz Band. There he met blues harmonica player Cyril Davies, with whom he launched the London Blues and Barrelhouse Club (1955) and started recording.

In 1961, Alexis declined to join a commercially promising skiffle band signed up by EMI executive George Martin. Instead, Korner and Davies formed Blues Incorporated, a loose-knit group of musicians with an affinity for electric blues. In late 1961, Brian Jones, a broadly built boy in a smart Italian suit, walked up to Korner and talked authoritatively about the blues. Brian wanted to play the Delta-style slide guitar in Korner's band.

On March 17, 1962, Blues Incorporated played in a new blues club in West London, Ealing. Shortly afterward Korner would receive a demo tape with three songs performed by a group from Dartford named Little Boy Blue and the Blue Boys. The tape was sent by a Mick Jagger. On the following Saturday Mick would perform Chuck Berry's "Around and Around" with Korner's band. Within a month, Mick had become Korner's second-string vocalist. The sad-faced part-time drummer of Blues Incorporated was a certain Charlie Watts, a student of commercial art in Harrow.

---

1 Most bios are heavily, but not exclusively, based on Wikipedia content.

Brian Jones

Lewis Brian Hopkins Jones was born in 1942 in Cheltenham, Gloucestershire. An attack of croup at the age of four left him with lifelong asthma. His middle-class parents were of Welsh descent. Brian had two sisters: Barbara and Pamela, who died of leukemia in 1945. His mother Louisa was a piano teacher, and his father was an aeronautical engineer who played piano and organ and led the local church choir. In 1957, Brian heard Cannonball Adderley, who inspired his interest in jazz. Brian persuaded his parents to buy him a saxophone, and two years later, his parents gave him his first acoustic guitar as a 17th birthday present.

Brian attended local schools. He enjoyed badminton and diving and played first clarinet in the school orchestra. Brian had an IQ of 135 and performed well in exams without much learning effort. However, he disliked school discipline, conforming, and the school uniforms. Brian annoyed his teachers but was popular with classmates; he was suspended from school twice. "He was a rebel without a cause, but when examinations came he was brilliant" (Dick Hattrell).

In 1959, Brian's 17-year-old girlfriend became pregnant. Brian encouraged her to have an abortion, but she carried the child to term and placed the baby for adoption. Brian quit school in disgrace and left home. During this period, he lived a bohemian lifestyle in Scandinavia, played guitar on the streets for money, and lived off the charity of others. When he ran short of money, Brian returned to England.

Brian listened to Elmore James and Robert Johnson, and he began performing at local blues and jazz clubs while working odd jobs. He stole money from work to pay for cigarettes, for which he was fired. In late 1959, Brian attended a concert in Guilford, where he met a young married woman named Angeline, who got pregnant after a one-night stand. She and her husband decided to raise the baby, but Brian never knew about the birth.

In 1961, Brian applied for a scholarship to Cheltenham Art College. The initial acceptance was withdrawn after a whistleblower denounced him as an irresponsible drifter. In October 1961, another girlfriend, Pat, gave birth to his third child, Julian Mark Andrews. Brian sold his record collection to buy flowers for Pat and clothes for the newborn. He lived with them for a while. In July 1964, another woman, Linda, gave birth to Brian's fourth child, Julian Brian. In late 1964, an occasional girlfriend of Brian's, Dawn, announced to Brian and the Stones' management that she was pregnant by Brian. Andrew Loog Oldham Ltd. paid her a check for £700 in exchange for silence.

In 1961, Brian moved to London and befriended Alexis Korner, Paul Jones (future singer of Manfred Mann's Earth Band), Jack Bruce, and others from the R&B and jazz scene there. He became a blues musician, played slide guitar, and called himself "Elmo Lewis." He started a group with Paul Jones called the "Roosters," which was in January 1963 joined by Eric Clapton after Brian's departure. Brian placed an advertisement in *Jazz News* inviting musicians to audition for a new R&B group at the Bricklayers Arms pub; Ian Stewart was the first to respond, followed by Mick and Keith. Brian and Ian accepted the Chuck Berry songs that Keith wanted to play, which triggered the departure of the band's blues purists Geoff Bradford and Brian Knight. The Rolling Stones played their first gig on July 12, 1962, in the Marquee Club with Mick, Brian, Ian, Keith, Dick Taylor on bass, and drummer Tony Chapman.

Brian enjoyed his celebrity as a pop star, with its dose of fame, attention, mobbing, clothes, money, girls, shopping, and nightclubs. However, with increasing stardom, Brian would become abusive. He mentally, financially, and physically abused both friends and girlfriends.

Brian did have songwriting ambitions but was too scared to put his songs forward. Andrew "realised that Brian did not love pop music, therefore he could not write it. ... Writing songs means one must pay attention to life, and Brian was loath to pay attention to anything but himself." Brian crucially lacked self-confidence. "I can identify myself with the group but I'm not sure about the image. This rebel thing has gone, now; life is a paradox for me. I'm so contradictory. I have this need for expression, but I'm not certain what it is I want to do. I'm not personally insecure, just unsure. ... I would like to write but I lack confidence and need encouragement." With Mick and Keith forging their songwriter alliance and gradual taking over the band leadership, Brian felt cast aside. His increasingly schizophrenic behavior and drug-induced underperformance ultimately estranged his band members and friends. "He formed the band. He chose the members. He named the band. He chose the music we played. He got us gigs. ... Very influential, very important, and then slowly lost it—highly intelligent—and just kind of wasted it and blew it all away" (Bill).

Reference must be made to Brian's collaboration in July 1968 with the Master Musicians of Joujouka, which culminated in the release of an album initially titled *Brian Jones Presents the Pipes of Pan at Joujouka*. The recording was made during an annual, weeklong festival in the honor of God Pan. The original album consisted of two uncut and unnamed tracks (one of each side of the Vinyl); the idea to link Sufi music to rock was wholly novel; and the whole project was extremely daring. It may have been the first-ever example of what would later be called "World Music."

Brian's voice can be heard distinctly singing backup on "Walking the Dog."

Ian Stewart

Ian was born in Kirklatch Farm, Scotland, in 1938 and raised in Sutton, Surrey. He learned piano at age six and loved boogie above all. "He blew my head off too, when he started to play. I never heard a white piano player play like that before" (Keith). Ian was first to respond to Brian's advertisement in *Jazz News* seeking musicians to form a rhythm and blues group. Stewart had a job at Imperial Chemical Industries (ICI). As none of the other Stones had a phone, Ian's desk at ICI was the headquarters of the Stones organization. He also bought a van to transport the group and their equipment to their gigs. Despite his seniority, Ian was ejected from the lineup because of his looks. Ian accepted this demotion by Andrew. "[Stu] might have realized that in the way it was going to have to be marketed, he would be out of sync, but that he could still be a vital part. I'd probably have said, 'Well, fuck you,' but he said 'OK, I'll just drive you around.' That takes a big heart, but Stu had one of the largest hearts around" (Keith). Ian refused to play in minor keys, saying, "When I'm on stage with the Stones and a minor chord comes along, I lift my hands in protest." He remained aloof from the band's lifestyle. "I think he looked upon it as a load of silliness. ... I also think it was because he saw what had happened to Brian. I could tell from the expression on his face when things started to get a bit crazy during the making of Exile on Main Street. I think he found it very hard. We all did" (Mick Taylor). Ian played golf and as road manager showed preference for hotels with courses. "We'd be playing in some town where there's all these chicks, and they want to get laid and we want to lay them. But Stu would have booked us into some hotel about ten miles out of town. You'd wake up in the morning and there's the links. We're bored to death looking for some action and Stu's playing Gleneagles" (Keith). Shortly after Stewart's unexpected death in 1986 Mick said, "Stu was the one guy we tried to please. We wanted his approval when we were writing or rehearsing a song. We'd want him to like it."

Michael Philip Jagger

Michael Philip Jagger was born in Dartford's Livingston Hospital on July 26, 1943, in the middle of World War II. During World War II, V-1 and V-2 missiles spread death and destruction in the Jaggers' immediate neighborhood. One of young Mick's earliest memories is watching his mother remove the blackout curtains from the windows in spring 1945.

Mick's father Basil Fanshawe "Joe" Jagger was born in 1913 as son of a village school headmaster. Joe had been educated in an "atmosphere of clean-living altruism." He studied physical training at Manchester and London universities and was appointed PT instructor at the state-run East Central School in Dartford, Kent. In 1947, Joe would take up an administrative position with the Central Council of Physical Recreation, the body overseeing all amateur sports associations throughout Britain. He became one of the nation's leading experts on basketball and devoted many unpaid hours to the coaching of the first Kent Council Basketball League. Later, the prestigious Catholic Strawberry Hill College would call on Joe to give conferences on baseball and to contribute to the formation of future PT teachers.

Joe met Eva Ensley Scutts in early 1940. The 27-year-old was as vivacious and demonstrative as Joe was understated and quiet. Eva was born in the same year as Joe, 1913, in Australia's New South Wales. Toward the end of the Great War, Eva's mother would leave her husband and move to Dartford with Eva and her four siblings. Eva felt ashamed of her birth in Down Under and assumed an exaggeratedly upper-class accent to hide any lingering Aussie twang, the reflex of an inferiority complex inherited from her London-born mother who had emigrated to Australia to marry an Australian shipbuilder. In Dartford, Eva and her mother would frequently travel to London to watch movies with Greta Garbo and other stars. During the depression years, Eva worked as a beautician and hairdresser. In the mid-1930s Eva would listen to big band swing and dance through the nights until she met Basil. They married in 1940 in Dartford's Holy Trinity Church, where Eva had sung in the choir. "My mother is a typical working-class specimen, and my father a bourgeois" (Mick).

In the postwar years, Mick and his younger brother Chris grew up in an atmosphere of security, comfort, and values. At his first school, Maypole Infants, Mick was a star pupil. Others would remember him as the brightest and most engaging boy in his year, a bundle of energy with a touch of the subversive. Mick liked to imitate his teachers. In *Olé Olé*, Mick tells how the family organized little stage shows in their living room where everyone had to impersonate somebody. This taught him not to be shy in public and to act out.

When Mick moved on to Wentworth County Primary, he met for the first time an "ill-favored fellow" with "protruding ears and hollow cheeks" born at the same hospital, Keith Richards.

At Jaggers', music was constantly in the air, and Mick enjoyed mimicking the American crooners he heard. While Mick had singing lessons at school and sang in the church choir, it was his brother Chris who won a prize for singing. Mick was most attracted by the musical entertainment shows with professional pantomimes. In 1954, the family moved from Dartford to Wilmington, to a secluded home called the Close. Joe would give his sons regular PT lessons in the spacious garden. The family went on vacation to Spain and France, but the boys were never spoiled. Joe was a "strict disciplinarian," and Eva was forceful over "cleanliness and tidiness" (Norman). Mick did his share of household work.

In 1955, Bill Haley's "Rock Around the Clock" shook up the proletarian dance halls. Dartford pupils, however, found Dave Brubeck's jazz much cooler. Early on, Mick got excited by Benny Goodman and Glenn Miller. Rock 'n' Roll was followed by a short-lived wave of skiffle, originally played by depression-area white folk from America with a touch of jazz. Band leader Chris Barber and banjo player Lonnie Donegan would make skiffle popular in Britain. Skiffle would turn the guitar from an "obscure back-row rhythm instrument into an object of young-manly worship" (Norman). Mick had a guitar but found it too hard to learn how to play it. Rather, with his organizational flair, he started a school record club, which made him discover falsetto-singing and rock 'n' roll, parroting Little Richard, the "first rock 'n' roller who made Mike Jagger forget all middle-class, grammar school sophistication and detachment, and surrender to the sheer mindless joy of music" (Norman). In 1958, Mick attended his first rock concert and enjoyed Buddy Holly's extrovert showmanship. Buddy played guitar solos while lying flat on his back, and Mick's favorite tune was "Not Fade Away." "This, Mick realized, was not just someone to copy, but to be" (Norman). Soon after, music forged a friendship across social boundaries between Mick and Dick Taylor, a plumber's son. Dick passed his passion for blues on to Mick. Unlike rock 'n' roll, blues did not just have a black subtext, it was "music wholly reflecting the experience of black people," a rarity in Britain then. Even finding blues records was difficult. Mick, Dick, and two other friends decided to form a blues band, Little Boy Blue, in which Mick was the vocalist. The aim was to celebrate the blues. Mick's "love for the blues was as passionate and sincere as he'd ever been about anything in his life" (Norman).

Mick nevertheless had another passion: he dreamed of becoming rich, not as an artist but as a businessman. Giving a boost to his high school studies, he finished among the best of his class and earned a scholarship to attend the London School of Economics (LSE).

After many years, Mick met Keith again on October 17, 1961, at Dartford train station. Mick was on his way to LSE, carrying *One Dozen Berry* records under his arm. Keith was on his way to Sidcup Art College, carrying his hollow-bodied Höfner cutaway electric guitar.

In March 1962, Alexis Korner's Blues Incorporated would play in a new blues club in West London, Ealing. Shortly afterward Korner would receive a demo tape with three songs performed by a group from Dartford named Little Boy Blue and the Blue Boys. The tape was sent by a Mick Jagger. On the following Saturday Mick would perform Chuck Berry's "Around and Around" with Korner's band. Korner noticed not so much the singing but the way the singer threw his hair around. After a moment of silence, there was a burst of applause for "someone whose love of blues could take him so far beyond the embarrassment barrier. The fact that he had copied Chuck Berry's phrasing note for note was further proof of being a true disciple" (Norman). Within a month, Mick had become Korner's second-string vocalist.

In spring 2000, Mick spoke at his old school in Dartford after donating money for the school's new swimming pool. "As Mick got up to speak ... it suddenly struck home that the guiding theme of his discourse was how it all had been accidental. There was no moral to his story except how easily it could have been otherwise" (Sandford). Shortly after, in May 2000, Mick's mother died at age 87. Friends say that with her combination of self-discipline, charm, and dogged social ambition, she had been *the* woman in Mick's life (Sandford).

In Charlie's view it was thanks to Mick's drive as a band leader that the Stones had been able to go on for such a long time. "Like any intelligent rock star, he found at least part of what he did ridiculous, and he desperately craved renewal."[2] "The private Mick Jagger emphasising hard graft, thrift and self-discipline juxtaposed uncomfortably with his public persona as, to many, a morally dissolute social rebel and, to others, a singing phallus. However, all those closest to him ... are insistent that behind the outer shell of rock-star glitz lay a vein of English traditionalism, or even romanticism."[3]

During a tour in Australia, Mick called his old Dartford school friend Paul Ovenden, who was driving a taxi in Melbourne. "He was quite unlike the image people have of him, and he talked a lot about his parents and cricket, and things we both missed in England." Paul mentioned that he was going through difficult times. "Mick gave me some advice about coping with it all

---

2 Sandford, *The Rolling Stones – Fifty Years*, 343.
3 Ibid., 302.

that I've never forgotten. The essence of it was 'integrity and perseverance.' The odd thing was, he said that in some ways he actually despised the rock-star life he lived himself."[4]

Mick had always remained close to his father Joe. When possible, Mick had his father attend his concerts, having him placed in a comfortable and secure position close to the soundboard opposite the stage. In October 2006, after the Stones played the New York Beacon Theatre in New York with Bill Clinton as MC (to be filmed by Martin Scorsese), the very night in which Ahmet Ertegun tripped over a cable and fell into a coma from which he would not wake up, Mick flew back to London to sit at the bedside of his frail father who had fallen recently and developed a pneumonia. Mick stayed a few days but then returned to the band, which was on tour. Mick had barely rejoined the band when he learned that Joe had passed way. Mick reportedly shed some tears. The Stones played their two-hour set as scheduled that night.

Keith Richards

Keith was born on December 18, 1943, at Livingston Hospital in Dartfort, Kent. Keith's father Bert was a quiet and cautious character who worked as supervisor at Osram's light bulb factory in Hammersmith, got up every day at 5:00 a.m., and would only return home at 6:00 p.m. "He'd have something to eat, watch TV for a couple of hours, then go to bed, absolutely knackered" (Keith). Keith grew up close to his mother, Doris, a warm and jolly woman. She had inherited their family's fondness for music and romance. As she did housework, the radio would constantly pour out American big band music. Her father, Theodore Augustus Dupree, of Huguenot origin, led a small semi-professional dance band in the 1930s and played several instruments including saxophone, violin, and guitar.

The Richardses lived in Chastilian Road, a street away from the Jaggers in Denver Road. Both Mick and Keith attended the Wentworth Primary School, where they met. When Keith asked Mick what he wanted to do when grown up, Mick replied he wanted to be a cowboy like Roy Rogers and play a guitar. "I wasn't that impressed by Roy Rogers, but the bit about the guitar did interest me" (Keith).

As a small boy, Keith sang soprano in the choir, and he performed in Westminster Abbey in the presence of the Queen.

---

4 Ibid., 369.

The Richardses moved to a small house in Spielman Road on the Temple Hill Estate. His mother picked up work in a baker's shop. Keith, "between his father's indifference and his mother's over-indulgence, began to resolutely go bad" (Norman). While he was talented in many respects, he totally lacked any sort of discipline. By the time he was 13, he was sent to Dartford Technical School.

When Doris bought Keith his first guitar, Keith would spend the day sitting at the top of the stairs playing it. Doris also saw to it that Keith learned to play it properly. It was the time of British rock 'n' roll. Tommy Steele and Terry Dene covered American songs that were released on Embassy Records and sold at Woolworth's. Keith began to copy them. However, he found that British rock was stale and that singers were accompanied by bored session men rather than an enthusiastic band. He started buying the American original records and fell for Elvis's guitarist Scotty Moore.

After being expelled from Dartford Technical School in 1958, Keith went to Sidcup Art College. "Sidcup Art College sounds immeasurably grander than it ever was. It existed, in fact, to give just such last chances to those whose inglorious school careers had fitted them for nothing better than what was then belittlingly called 'commercial art'" (Norman). At Sidcup, Keith was introduced to authentic blues music.

One morning, on the way from Dartford to Sidcup, Keith bumped into Mick, who held a pile of imported blues albums purchased from Chess Records by mail order under his arm. Mick was playing in the band Little Boy Blue at that time, with common friend Dick Taylor, and invited Keith to join.

In the meantime, Keith had learned to play almost all Chuck Berry licks, including "Johnny B Goode." "He understood that even this complex break, like two guitars in unison, required something more than simply playing notes fast" (Norman). "Keith sounded great—but he wasn't flash. ... When he came in, you could feel something holding the band together" (Dick Taylor). Little Boy Blue continued to play R&B music with Dick's mother as only audience. One day they played for a snap show. "The snap shows Dick and Keith with their guitars parodying Chuck Berry's duck walk, and Mick Jagger in his student's button-up cardigan, striking a dramatic pose against the background of drainpipe and pebbledash council house wall" (Norman).

The best way to get to know Keith is to read the great biography by Victor Bockris and to watch *Under the Influence*, the incredibly insightful Netflix production. It shows Keith as a tender person and a musical archaeologist who is well-connected to the "higher spheres."

Artistically, Keith views himself as a medium. "Songs are funny things. They wake you in the middle of the night. ... They control you. ... I don't think

I write 'em, I think I receive them" (Keith). Even in recent times Keith has played his guitar every day, to see whether some song is finding its way to him. In the bonus section of Scorsese's *Shine a Light*, Keith can be seen picking his guitar introvertedly in a corner of the stage, while Mick is chatting mundanely with the Clintons.

Bockris describes Keith's spiritual journey. In the 1990s Keith began declaring that whenever the Stones play outdoor, God is a member of the band. He launched the "Wingless Angels" to record two albums of Rasta roots gospel songs "to pay dues" not only to reggae but to the Lord himself. On *Bridges to Bremen* he can be heard greeting the audience with the words "God bless you." In *Olé Olé* a scene shows how Keith performs his usual small ritual with his magic wand on stage during the sound check preceding the show so as to avoid rain. When it once rained despite his ritual, Keith commented with a quirky smile: "Well, it does not always work."

Privately, Keith is a family man. "The only way you can be like me is to have a good family" (Keith). He also likes children: "They do more for you than you do for them" (Keith).

When called to his mother's deathbed, Keith sat at her bedside during the entirety of her last night, playing the guitar. When his mom woke up, he asked whether she had heard him play. She replied yes and that he had been out of tune.

Charlie Watts

Charles Robert "Charlie" Watts was born in 1941 to Charles Watts, a lorry driver for a precursor of British Rail, and his wife Lilian (née Eaves) in London. He was raised (along with his sister Linda) in Kingsbury. Charlie attended Tylers Croft Secondary Modern School from 1952 to 1956; as a schoolboy, he displayed a talent for art, cricket, and football.

As a child, Charlie Watts and his family lived in a prefabricated home, as did many in the community. Watts' earliest records were jazz recordings, 78 RPM vinyls of Jelly Roll Morton and Charlie Parker. At about age 13, Watts became interested in drumming. A jazzman, Watts initially found his transition to R&B puzzling: "I went into rhythm and blues. When they asked me to play, I didn't know what it was. I thought it meant Charlie Parker played slow." After completing secondary school, he enrolled at Harrow Art School, which he attended until 1960. After leaving school, Watts worked as a graphic designer for an advertising company called Charlie Daniels Studios and played drums occasionally with local bands in coffee shops and clubs. In 1961, he met

Alexis Korner who invited him to join his band, Blues Incorporated. Watts played regularly with Blues Incorporated and maintained a job with another advertising firm of Charles Hobson and Grey. It was in mid-1962 that Watts first met Brian, Ian, Mick, and Keith, but it wasn't until January 1963 that Watts finally agreed to join the Rolling Stones. In 1964, Watts married Shirley Ann Shepherd, whom he had met before the band became successful. They were still married when Charlie passed away.

In the early 1980s, Charlie struggled emotionally after the early death of his father and other family issues and started using alcohol, amphetamines, and even heroin. He was reluctant to go on tour. "Should I really tour? All that hassle. All that hard work. All those terrible arse-lickers. The only reason I could go through with it is that it's better than the fucking alternative" (Charlie).

Charlie followed Keith's advice that going on stage is the best therapy. "You can be feeling like dog-shit, and within five minutes you're cured" (Keith).

Throughout his life with the Stones, Charlie engaged in many jazz projects. Not very talkative, Charlie became a stabilizing factor in the complex interpersonal relationships between the band members over the years, and he has been increasingly recognized as such. Privately, Charlie lived in Dolton, a rural village in Devon, where he raised Arabian horses. Charlie also collected Civil War memorabilia. In 2006, Vanity Fair elected him into the *International Best Dressed List Hall.*

The best way to understand Charlie's professionalism is to watch a short video named "Charlie's Drum Kit."[5]

Charlie is a master in understatement. When the Stones played at Twickenham Stadium in September 2003, Charlie gave an interview to BBC's Charlie Gillett and afterward sent him a handwritten thank you note signed with his name and the words "Drummer for the Rolling Stones."

In the beginning of August 2021, Charlie had to step down from the 2021 tour for medical reasons. He did so with his usual grace and humor in very few words, designing himself his successor. On August 24, 2021, the media surprised the world by announcing Charlie's passing.

By the time of his death, Charlie had created a wonderful legacy and given joy to millions of people.

---

5 https://www.youtube.com/watch?v=7PZug4854sI.

Bill Wyman

Bill Wyman was born in 1936 in South London, the son of William Perks, a bricklayer, and his wife Molly. One of five children, Wyman spent most of his early life living in one of the roughest streets in Sydenham, southeast London. He describes his childhood as "scarred by poverty." Bill is one of the most accomplished bassists and a master in the art of musical understatement. Together with Keith and Charlie, Bill formed the best ever rhythm section of rock 'n' roll, and his rolling and dancing bass lines excel in the art of counterpoint. On stage, Bill would just stand still in a corner, "lay back and fatten up the sound" (it is thus with irony that he was credited with "bass and dancing" on the cover sleeves of *Love You Live*, the Stones' 1977 live album). Following Bill's playing with the Stones requires active listening. Whenever the bass is prominent in the mix, it is a strong indication that either Keith or Ron has taken over the instrument. From early on, Bill expressed frustration that his songs were not deemed worthy for the Stones' albums. When the Stones released *Their Satanic Majesties Request* in December 1967, the biggest surprise was to find a song by Bill Wyman among the ten tracks, "In Another Land." Bill had been the only Stone on time in the Studio, and he used his chance. Later Mick and Keith worked on the track and agreed to putting it on the album. However, Mick asked Bill for a share in the publishing rights as compensation for the production work. "Then the news that someone else in the band wrote songs was kept jealously under wraps. On the album credits it was attributed to 'the Rolling Stones'; only on its American release as a single did Bill get an individual credit" (Norman). When Bill announced his intention to quit, one of the reasons advanced was that he had developed a fear of flying. But Bill had other long-standing artistic grievances. "Fuck you lot, you didn't use any of my songs." Keith replied: "Haven't you sussed that they're useless songs?" Another song penned by Bill was released on *Metamorphosis*, in 1975. The song "Downtown Suzie" is well-built and actually quite humorous.

Bill eventually left in 1994. According to many, his departure affected the Stones' sound more than the departure of Brian or Mick Taylor.

Giorgio Gomelsky

Giorgio Gomelsky, born in Tiflis in 1934, was a Russian émigré exiled from Georgia to Switzerland, educated in Italy and Germany. He had helped Chris Barber to set up the National Jazz League. The Stones had played in his Piccadilly Club, but Giorgio found their playing abominable. After the closure of the club, Giorgio found a new venue in the backroom of the Station Hotel in Kew Road, Richmond, called the Crawdaddy after Bo Diddley's song "Do the Crawdaddy." Its first resident attraction for the Sunday night shows (7:00 to 10:30 p.m.) was the Dave Hunt Group featuring Ray Davies (later with the Kinks), a band that played in Louis Jordan's 1940s jump band style. When the group could not make one gig due to snow, Giorgio rang up Ian Stewart. "Tell everyone in the band you guys are on next Sunday." That first night the attendance was so much reduced that Giorgio went through the surrounding pubs offering half-price tickets. But within weeks the band had attracted a huge following, of which R&B enthusiasts were only the minor part. There were mods, rockers, art students, and middle-class youth. Initially, the crowd was merely standing and watching, until Giorgio's assistant Hamish Grimes "jumped on a tabletop and began to leap and flail his arms with the music like a dervish." From that impromptu outburst evolved a twist-like dance peculiar to the Crawdaddy Club that could be performed by couples and singles alike. The 20-minute dancing frenzy became the ritual-like climax of each Stones session. From then on, Giorgio would give the band a lot of support, without ever trying to secure exclusivity as a manager. On the contrary, his advice was to let no one have control over them but themselves. Being in contact with the Beatles' Brian Epstein, he invited the Beatles to the Crawdaddy a night when the Stones were performing. When Giorgio returned from a trip to Switzerland, the Stones had signed a three-year exclusive management contract with Andrew Oldham and Eric Easton.

Giorgio was the perfect incarnation of the selfless helping hand.

Andrew Oldham

Andrew Loog Oldham, born in 1944 as the son of a Dutch American air force officer killed in a mission over Germany, was in search of glamor and fame. A PR assignment for American record producer Phil Spector altered his conception of the music business. Phil Spector was the first producer to be as famous as his performing acts. From then on Andrew wanted to become another Phil. In April 1963, Andrew went to see the Stones at the Crawdaddy. Giorgio was in Switzerland burying his father, and that night the club atmosphere was morbid. The Stones would do their blues roots thing, sitting on a ring of bar stools in a morbid atmosphere. He intuitively felt their potential. Andrew knew he was not able to manage a pop group on his own; he went to see Brian Epstein and proposed a deal whereby Epstein could have 50 percent of the Rolling Stones. Epstein felt he was too busy and declined. Andrew was more lucky with music agent Eric Easton. Both went to see the Stones at the Crawdaddy. While Easton pondered strategy, Andrew tried to get intimate with the Stones, pretending to share their mission to bring pure blues and R&B to a wider audience.

The following three years, Andrew would push the Stones to frequently release new albums on both sides of the Atlantic following different editorial policies, frequently with sub-satisfactory material lacking consistency in musical policy, a mix of pop and R&B tracks. Andrew would pursue his branding efforts through his infamous back cover liner notes that caused uproar and scandal in the media. A Conservative member of the House of Lords would ask the director of public prosecutions to investigate this "deliberate incitement to criminal action."

Andrew quit in 1967.

Dick Rowe

Dick Rowe of Decca Records, born 1921, was known as the man who turned the Beatles down. His sole consolation was that no pop group would last longer than six months. Now he was looking for the next Beatles up in the North, attending a talent show in Liverpool's Philharmonic Hall. Rowe watched the Stones in the Crawdaddy, but following A&R protocol, he tried to find out who was managing them by calling around his usual contacts. Nobody had ever heard of the Stones, but eventually someone said, "Try Eric Easton." A deal was made within days.

Allen Klein

Allen Klein was born in 1932 in Newark, the son of a kosher butcher. After his mother's early death, the father would put him and his sister into the Hebrew Shelter Orphanage. Allen Klein studied to become an accountant, and he was known for his enormous working capacity. Allen "specialised in obtaining large advance payments for recording artists." When taking on teenage pop singer Buddy Knox, Allen discovered that his record company had withheld significant amounts of royalties. He managed to obtain them for his client. Allen's pitch was straightforward: "I can find you money you never knew you even had." His technique was to harass the record company with an avalanche of legal writs. "If a corporation is big, it *has* to make mistakes" (Emphasis in original). After unsuccessful career attempts in the movie business, Allen concentrated on the pop music industry. In 1964, Allen approached the Beatles'

Brian Epstein to propose Klein's Sam Cooke as opening act. He also proposed to Epstein to manage the Beatles' finances. Epstein declined respectfully. Klein was more successful with Mickie Most, the Animals, Herman's Hermits and Donovan. And, unfortunately, with the Stones.

When Klein struck his deal with the Stones, Klein would take over the financial side, and Andrew kept the creative parts of his job. Klein struck a great deal with Decca, but he channeled funds into his own company, which led to a fallout. He also took over the management of the Beatles but never gained Paul McCartney's trust, who preferred his father-in-law, Lee Eastman, to run the Beatles' affairs.

Klein's biggest scoop, highly detrimental to the Stones, was to walk away with the rights to the entire song catalog of the early years (1963–1969).

Prince Rupert Loewenstein

Prince Rupert Ludwig Ferdinand zu Loewenstein-Wertheim-Freudenberg was born in Palma, Mallorca, in 1933 as the son of Prince Leopold zu Loewenstein-Wertheim-Freudenberg and his wife, Countess Bianca Treuberg. Prince Rupert's father, Prince Leopold zu Loewenstein-Wertheim-Freudenberg, descended from a family that can be traced back to Luitpold Margrave of Carinthia and later duke of Bavaria, who died repelling the Huns in 907. "Tenue was my father's touchstone" (Loewenstein). His mother was Countess Bianca Treuberg from Bavaria. Prince Leopold described himself a Catholic but was also interested in Oriental and Egyptian religions.

After his parents' separation, Prince Rupert's mother sent him to St. Christopher School where Quakerism was blended with the views of the Theosophical Society. As a student in Cambridge, Prince Rupert was influenced by Father Alfred Gilbey, chaplain to Cambridge University, a traditionalist Catholic who celebrated the Old Catholic Mass. In Cambridge he also met the Belgian Benedictine monk Father Dominique de Gunne, who would later become Belgian King Baudouin's private tutor. He taught Rupert his maxim "pas de sentimentalité." As the family had no money, Prince Rupert soon learned that the world of medieval castles, governesses, tutors, and liveried servants was based on very weak financial foundations. After studying medieval history at Magdalen College in Oxford, he became a stockbroker for Bache & Co. In 1963, he formed a consortium with friends to buy the merchant bank Leopold Joseph & Sons, which had its roots in Michelstadt in the German Odenwald.

Mick met Prince Rupert a few weeks after he had recommended Allen Klein to John Lennon. Mick rang Lennon back to correct the shot, but it was too late. After Mick, Rupert met the other Stones. "I saw that Keith was in a way—and I hesitate to say this—the most intelligent mind of all the band." After their arrival in French tax exile, Prince Rupert spotted a pile of LPs in Keith's barely unpacked boxes, Johann Sebastian Bach's 48 Preludes and Fugues. Prince Rupert got along well with Mick and Keith, understanding their competitive relationship.

His work with the Stones would form part of what would become a new way for bands to do business. Due to his connections in international society, Prince Rupert opened many doors for the Stones. His services ranged from identifying innovative business opportunities to sorting out immigration and visa problems for the Stones, whose drug convictions created frequent obstacles to international travel. Prince Rupert was also one of the first business managers to develop an international tax strategy in the entertainment industry that would overarch and determine the movements and investments of the band. He urged the Stones to leave the UK, sell their properties in the UK, and acquire real estate in France and elsewhere, and even Mick's acquisition of an abode on the fashionable island of Mustique was driven by fiscal considerations. A relative of Prince Rupert had acquired Mustique and developed it, negotiating a special tax status for the island. He offered the first developed lot to Princess Margaret to attract other affluent clients.

Prince Rupert innovated touring, introduced corporate "meets and greets," and educated the Stones about cost management. Prince Rupert also advised Cat Stevens on managing the problem of forbidden interest payments after Steven's conversion to Islam. "We had several rather difficult meetings about this, because one of the things we had done was to arrange for the bank to pay him a fixed, though higher, amount of money against his royalties for a longer period of time before he would enjoy the basic capital sum at the end of the period." Prince Rupert also ensured that a certain percentage of profits from each tour were given to charitable organizations. Despite his stature as president of the British Association of the Sovereign Military Order of Malta, an ancient Catholic order of 1,000 years, Prince Rupert saw some of his donations rejected by Catholic clergy. From time to time, he would cause the Stones to amend lyrics or elements of the staging to avoid clashes with local religious sensibilities.

Married to Josephine Lowry-Corry, a trained ballerina and opera singer, both of the couple's sons, Konrad and Rudolf, became Catholic priests, Konrad a traditionalist one. Prince Rupert, who was also Grand Inquisitor of the Constantinian Military Order of St. George and president of the Order of the Knights of Malta, never had problems reconciling faith and work in the godless world of rock 'n' roll. "On medieval pilgrimages, I later learnt, pilgrims had to put up with repetitive, rather dull drumming, a constant quasi-musical noise all the time. Rock and roll has its precursors."

The Stones are well aware of what they owe Prince Rupert: "And there's Rupert. He is a great financial mind for the market. He plays that like I play guitar. He does things like a little oilwell. And currency—you know, Swiss francs in the morning, switch to marks in the afternoon, move to the yen, and by the end of the day, how many dollars? That's his financial genius, his wisdom. Little pieces of paper. As long as there's a smile on Rupert's face, I'm cool" (Keith).[6]

Prince Rupert retired from the Stones in 2007 after failing to broker a takeover of the Stones by an "interested individual." In fact, at a time when the Stones reached age 65, he proposed to sell the band's assets to an investor and wind down their touring and playing careers. Thus, he proposed retirement, a move that was immediately rejected by the other band members. While the parting was amicable, Mick did not appreciate the level of financial disclosure in Prince Rupert's highly interesting memoirs. Like the great Moses, Prince Rupert stumbled over one incident and was barred from entering the Holy Land.

While the Stones have brought their talent to the table, their wealth and long-term financial success are largely due to the ingenuity of Prince Rupert. He died in 2014.

Ahmet Ertegun

Born in Istanbul in 1923 to an aristocratic Turkish family, Ahmet moved to Washington, D.C., in 1935, where his father served as the first ambassador of the Republic of Turkey to the United States. Ahmet's mother was an accomplished musician who played keyboard and stringed instruments. She bought the popular records of the day, which Ahmet listened to. At the age of 14, his mother bought him a record-cutting machine, which he used to compose and add lyrics to instrumental records. Ahmet's love for music pulled him into the heart of Washington, D.C.,'s black district where he would routinely see acts such as Duke Ellington, Cab Calloway, Billie Holiday, Louis Armstrong, and countless others. "I began to discover a little bit about the situation of

---

6 Andy Serwer, Julia Boorstin, and Ann Harrington, "Inside the Rolling Stones Inc," *Fortune Magazine*, September 30, 2002.

black people in America and experienced immediate empathy with the victims of such senseless discrimination, because, although Turks were never slaves, they were regarded as enemies within Europe because of their Muslim beliefs."

In 1946, Ahmet Ertegun became friends with Herb Abramson, an A&R man for National Records, and they decided to start a new independent record label for gospel, jazz, and R&B music. Financed by family dentist Dr. Vahdi Sabit, they formed Atlantic Records in September 1947, and the first recording sessions took place that November. Atlantic helped challenge the primacy of the major labels of the time by discovering, developing, and nurturing new talent. It became the premier rhythm and blues label in just a few years and, with the help of innovative engineer/producer Tom Dowd, set new standards in producing high-quality recordings. In 1957, Atlantic was among the first labels to record in stereo and, in 1958, introduced four tracks and later eight tracks of taped multi-track recording.

In the 1960s, Atlantic's partnerships with local labels like Stax Records (Memphis) helped to develop the growth of soul music, with artists such as Solomon Burke, Otis Redding, Percy Sledge, Aretha Franklin, and Wilson Pickett. Ahmet heard a demo of Led Zeppelin and immediately knew they would be a smash hit; he quickly signed them. After signing Crosby, Stills, and Nash, Ertegun convinced the trio to allow Neil Young to join them on one of their tours, thereby founding Crosby, Stills, Nash, and Young. Ahmet eventually sold Atlantic to Warner Brothers in 1967 for $17 million in stock. When Atlantic became part of the Kinney conglomerate in 1969, and later part of Time Warner, Atlantic Records continued with Ahmet Ertegun at the helm, and although he was less directly involved as a producer, he wielded considerable influence in the new conglomerate.

At the age of 83 on October 29, 2006, Ahmet attended the Stones' benefit concert at the Beacon Theatre for the Clinton Foundation, which was attended by former US president Bill Clinton and his family. This is the concert filmed by Martin Scorsese (*Shine a Light*). Backstage in a VIP zone called "Rattlesnake Inn," Ahmet tripped and fell, striking his head on the concrete floor. He was immediately rushed to hospital but slipped into a coma and died weeks later on December 14, 2006, with his family by his side. Ahmet was buried on December 18 in the Garden of Sufi Tekke in Istanbul.

Up to his death, Ahmet and his wife liked to party wild and hard with their rock 'n' roll friends, with Ahmet being impeccably dressed in a three-piece. When a journalist once asked whether he did not sometimes feel "out of place," Ahmet replied, "Better out of place than out of character."

Promogroup B.V.

The Stones have several income streams with different business models run by different people that look after them. Connected to the Stones partnership and the late Prince Rupert is a group of companies that include Promotour, Promopub, Promotone, and Musidor, each dedicated to a particular aspect of the business. Mick ensures that everything is interlocked. These companies are based in the Netherlands for fiscal reasons.

According to the commercial registry, Promogroup B.V. is an Amsterdam-based holding company owned by the Rolling Stones, active since 1972. The company holds many of the band's copyrights and is often listed under ℗ and © credits. It also owns Rolling Stones Records and Musidor N.V. It manages the wealth of Mick, Keith, and Charlie. In 2006, Ron was not eligible to have his assets managed by Promogroup as he had "only" £70 million in the bank.

Over the 1990–2006 period, Promogroup reportedly arranged tax shelters that allowed the three band members to pay only $7.2 million taxes on revenues from royalties (not including tour income) totaling $450 million, that is, a tax rate of 1.5 percent. The Netherlands are in fact a preferred jurisdiction for income derived from intellectual property, as royalties are not taxed. This tax shelter drew media attention after U2 moved its own tax shelter from Ireland to Amsterdam to have it managed by Johannes Favie, the accountant who runs Promogroup. Fan Curtis, then Stones spokeswoman, declined to comment as the band members "don't like to talk about their business," but in a legal matter in the United States, Mick confirmed that "the recording services of the Rolling Stones are provided by companies that have the right to such services to Promotone B.V., which in turn owns the recordings of the Rolling Stones; my understanding is that Promotone licenses exploitation of those recordings to EMI Music Netherlands B.V., which releases and distributes those recordings through other companies in the United States."[7]

In 2006, after his fall from a tree in Fiji, Keith, Charlie, and Mick turned to Johannes Favie to set up a pair of private Dutch foundations that would allow them to transfer assets tax-free to heirs.

For the purpose of rebutting the allegation, made in 2017 following the release of the Panama Papers, of being just a letterbox company, Promogroup published a statement in Dutch, here translated mainly by Google Translate, with the following self-characterization:

---

7 Lynnley Browning, NY Times, February 4, 2007.

Since 1972, Promogroup is the owner—and not just the licensee—of the worldwide IP rights in relation to the band "The Rolling Stones." At the end of the sixties, the band ran into trouble with its manager at that time. For that reason, and partly because of record-high taxes in England during that period, the band left England. The company was established in the Netherlands partly because of the IP expertise, the infrastructure and stable legislation present there. Promogroup is exclusively engaged in the exploitation and protection of the IP rights created by the band, which Promogroup directly owns. In terms of exploitation, Promogroup is engaged in the administrative tasks of producing and releasing albums, including making payments to the many persons and organizations that provide services for Promogroup for a shorter or longer period. All in all, Promogroup carries out numerous factual activities. It is supervising projects such as recording albums, producing DVDs and, documentaries, as well as the compilation of books. ... It operates and manages the global portfolio of brands, including the well-known "tongue & lip" logo and the "The Rolling Stones" brand. It acts against frequent infringements of the band's trademark portfolio. It processes requests regarding the use of the band's rights by third parties. It concludes licensing agreements in relation to recording, publishing, authoring, DVD/film, image & likeness, merchandising and neighboring rights; ... it collects royalties and analyses royalty statements and it performs royalty audits at record companies, publishing companies and collecting societies. It also deals with third parties such as co-writers, producers and former band members and conducts the administration and financial management of all group companies. Furthermore, Promogroup owns and controls the UK-based archive of the band, which contains equipment, stage items, tour props, musical instruments. Above all the archive contains all master recordings from past decades (in conditioned spaces), including audio-visual recordings (films and concert recordings) and audio recordings (albums and studio sessions). These recordings are presently being digitized under the direction of Promogroup, including for the purpose of creating new releases (for example, an anniversary release of the album "Sticky Fingers" to which previously unreleased tracks will be added), which is a big project. The archive is also used for the current touring exhibition "Exhibitionism" (currently in Chicago).

In order to properly exploit and monitor its IP rights, Promogroup uses a number of subsidiaries as practical vehicles as a result of administrative and risk allocation considerations. For example, Musidor B.V. holds the trademarks and the portrait rights of the band members. Another example is Promotone B.V., which owns the master recordings and neighboring rights. Yet another example is Promopub B.V., which owns the music pub-lishing rights. … Promogroup is not a trust office, it does not have a trust license, does not use a trust office and is not managed by a trust office. … It should be clear that Promogroup—with real economic activities for itself and its shareholders … does not qualify as a trust office. Promogroup is not a … "letterbox company." … Promogroup also maintains a physical and real office at Herengracht 566 in Amsterdam. … In view of its activi-ties in relation to the exploitation and protection of IP rights, Promogroup is an active company with employees that pays tax in the Netherlands in accordance with the legal rules and rates. Promogroup has a management board residing in the Netherlands and a Board of Supervisory directors, one of the two members living in the Netherlands and the other in the United Kingdom (she is the manager of the Rolling Stones). Promogroup has 5 FTE staff. Like every company established in the Netherlands, Promogroup pays corporate tax and withholds payroll taxes on the salary of employees. Promogroup is not part of an international group but is the parent company of a group based in the Netherlands. … Promogroup has no agreements with the tax authorities. … In conclusion, Promogroup is a company with employees and real activities. As a company of and for the Rolling Stones, Promogroup has been established in the Netherlands since 1972 because of its excellent infrastructure, expertise and a stable political climate. … Promogroup is nothing more and nothing less than a company that exploits and protects its IP rights. … Hopefully the interrogation of Promogroup will contribute to your insight into its activities and activities and a solution to the persistent misunderstanding that Promogroup uses.

Ronnie Wood

Ronnie was born on June 1, 1947, in Hillingdon, Middlesex, into a family of traveling barge people (so-called water gypsies) and grew up in Western London. His father played in a harmonica orchestra and his older brothers were both accomplished musicians and graphic designers. Ronnie from early on experimented with both arts.

After a few short stints in short-lived bands, he joined the first Jeff Beck Group as a bassist in 1967, with Rod Stewart on vocals and Nicky Hopkins on piano. Two years later, he and Rod joined the Small Faces after Steve Marriott's departure. The band would change its name to Faces, and Ron played the guitar ever since.

The Small Faces were one of the big mod acts in the 1960s, and while less charismatic on stage than the Who, they created a more blues-rooted legacy.

The Faces, however, did not maintain that level of quality. Their studio record-ings lack catchy songs and overall bite and so do their live recordings. Maybe both Rod and Ron viewed the Faces as a simple and transitory career step. The Faces disintegrated over an unspecified period with Rod launching his solo career and Ron developing his own projects and moving closer to the Stones. Kenney Jones would replace the late Keith Moon in the Who, and Ian McLagan would serve as keyboard to both the Who and the Stones. Ronnie Lane died of multiple sclerosis, not without receiving much empathic support from music colleagues including Charlie Watts and Ron Wood (*Mahoney's Last Stand*), which produced beautiful results, such as the collaboration with Pete Townshend *Rough Mix*.

When listening to Faces albums, Ronnie's signature style is already pre-sent, but he had not yet matured to his full potential. When he replaced Mick Taylor, first unofficially on "Black 'n Blue" and as a band member during the 1975/1976 tour, a certain skepticism prevailed in the fan community. Would he be at the level of departed Mick? At that time, rock acts still derived credibility from virtuoso guitarists. The longer and faster a solo, the better it was received. Ronnie was clearly not at the same level of virtuosity as Mick T. Further, while Mick T. had that introverted touch—celebrating music with an angelic atti-tude—Ronnie displayed a rather clownish behavior: in a certain way, he desa-cralized the lead guitarist mystique prevailing in the early 1970s. Yet he would gradually reveal a different type of mastery. On *Love You Live*, it is easy to dis-tinguish his bubbling guitar style from Keith's rough chords, but on the subse-quent *Some Girls*, both guitars are blended so that it is difficult to figure out who plays which part. An exception to the rule is the dobro, slide and pedal steel solos on "Shattered" (a punk song with country and reggae riffs) or "Faraway Eyes." Over the years, Ronnie's guitar style evolved through progressive reduc-tion. He would play fewer and fewer notes, but each of them with an ever-bigger halo and expressively sculpted. Ronnie is a gifted storyteller when he speaks, but he tells his most beautiful stories through his guitar play, and not one of his notes is boring. In fact, Ronnie has long been one of the most underrated guitar heroes. Did he deliberately hold back as a guitarist to allow Keith to recover from the intimidation Keith had suffered during the Taylor-era?

Ronnie is also a superior songwriter. He has an impressive number of solo records, some of which are very good, including *I've Got My Own Album to Do*, *Gimme Some Neck*, *Slide on This*, and *I Feel Like Playing*. Musically, they are at par with, if not above, the solo efforts of both Mick and Keith.

Although Ronnie made equity in the Stones around 1990 as far as touring income is concerned, he does not share in royalty income from songwriting.

In his documentary *Somebody Up There Likes Me*, he comments on financial inequality in the Rolling Stones: "That as well is part of rock 'n' roll."

Over the years, Ronnie developed his painting. One of his art books was called *Wood on Canvas*. Sales of his pictorial works complement his income as a musician. In *Olé Olé*, Ron reveals another motivation behind his painting efforts: when painting he enjoys "being in control," with no one telling him what to do.

Ron also had some very expensive habits, cocaine and alcohol. When tested for the big tours following the resurrection of the Stones in 1989, he once exceeded the tolerated level of alcohol consumption by a factor of 17. Now sober, he told Keith that he is just as happy as before. Keith allegedly replied something like "So you spent 20 million for nothing!"

Like Mick and Keith, Ronnie came to realize his blessings over the years. In "Worried No More," the opening song of his first album after joining the Stones, *Gimme Some Neck*, Ron celebrates not having to fear the devil anymore. It is not entirely clear how exactly he meant it. In his autobiographical documentary *Somebody Up There Likes Me*, we can hear Ronnie add "... and somebody down here likes me too." When diagnosed with lung cancer in 2017, Ronnie refused chemotherapy because he did not want to lose his hair. In his recent documentary, he also tells how his remaining lung has miraculously recovered from the disease.

Ronnie has another important quality: that of being a reliable friend. For decades, he has been a close friend of Rod Stewart but also of Bob Dylan, who wrote "Seven Days" especially for Ron. Ron supported Bob on the Dylan albums recorded during Bob's much-criticized Christian phase.

If the Stones survived as a band, Ron played a significant role in this. First, as Keith's drinking buddy with a talent for self-derision, he allowed Keith to recover his self-confidence as a guitarist. Second, Ron (re)introduced humor to the Stones. Third, he frequently mediated between Mick and Keith in their feuds. Admittedly he had a personal interest in the survival of the Stones, but that does not diminish his efforts. Fourth, his vinegar-style slide guitar licks brought the Stones sound closer to the dissonant bluesy touch of their earlier days. During the 1978 and 1981/1982 tours, Ron excelled in taking Keith's original concept of "guitar weaving" to unprecedented heights.

"The Rolling Stones"

In the beginning, the *Rolling Stones* were simply a music band. "The whole joy of making rock 'n' roll music is the interaction between guys playing" (Keith).

A band is a group of people playing together. "Most people don't know what a band is. The musicians are there to contribute to the band's sound. The band isn't there for showing off solos or egos." (Keith). This brings about constraints and joys. "The whole joy of making rock 'n' roll music is the interaction between guys playing" (Keith).

A band that lasts as long as the *Rolling Stones* brings its own challenges for its members, who had to realize at some point that they were bound to be part of that collective entity for virtually all of their lifetime. Fortunately, the way the *Rolling Stones* evolved left sufficient time and money for the band members to explore individual artistic paths and to enjoy leisurely activities. Artistically, however, the *Rolling Stones* were more and better than their individual members.

Keith has always been a strong supporter of band philosophy. "There's no way you can say that any one person is the band and the rest are just padding. It is such a subtle mixture of characters and personalities and how you deal with each other. ... Coca-Cola know[s] what the ingredients are. We only know there is four guys ... very different people... but the chemistry is there" (Keith).

This does not mean automatic alignment and harmonious homogeneity. "They almost talk to each other in grunts, because there are so many different personalities that don't get on naturally, when they're together. It's 'We're the Rolling Stones so we gotta put this act on,' and they literally become more than the sum of their parts. I said to Jagger, 'I just can't handle it when you guys are all together. It's just depressing.' He said, 'I know, you're right'" (Nick Kent).[8]

Over the years, the *Rolling Stones* gradually emerged as a distinct persona, with a personality clearly separate from their individual members and more than the sum of the individuals: "We're just a bunch of extremely different guys who are going off at extremely different tangents. The Rolling Stones is a vehicle that only works when we actually put it into motion" (Ronnie). In an interview with a magazine, Rolling Stone following the end of the "No Filter Tour," Steve Jordan expressed exactly this: "The Stones are like a thing unto themselves. Even the band members, when they talk about the Stones, it's like they're talking about something else. They'll be like, 'The Stones were

---

8 Bockris, *Keith*, 188.

doing this,' and I'm like, 'You're in the Stones!' It's like this third person, or something."[9]

The solo projects of the various Stones members reveal a taste for variety in styles, tenderness, and sweetness, in stark contrast to the Kali-like multiheaded beast that consumes and devours its children (Brian, Graham Parsons, Andy Johns, Jimmy Miller, Mick Taylor, Anita Pallenberg, Marianne Faithfull, Meredith Hunter, and more).

There is also an increasing awareness, at least as concerns Keith, that the *Rolling Stones* are destined to play a prophetic role in channeling down positive energies from the higher spheres for the benefit of humankind ("I'm only a vessel"). At one point Keith explained his roles in words along the following lines (quoted from memory): "I receive an idea, I put it into form that others can understand, and I pass it on." Music being a "necessity of life" (Keith), the *Rolling Stones* are particularly talented at supplying it. "You've got the sun, you've got the moon, and you've got the Rolling Stones" (Keith). Keith also believes that the *Rolling Stones* are not alone when they play outdoors. "You're relying on God, who joins the band every night in one form or another" (Keith), be it rain, wind, or snow. However, the *Rolling Stones* never pretended to be Godlike. Rather, they view themselves as disciples in the service of the Afro-American blues. "It's probably the most important thing that America has ever given to the world" (Keith). While the blues started about some hundred to hundred and fifty years ago, "the music is about a feeling, and feelings didn't just start a hundred years ago. Feelings start in the person, and I think that's why the blues is universal, because it's part of everybody" (Keith). Thus, the *Rolling Stones* pass on the tradition they received. "What Muddy Waters did for us is what we should do for others" (Keith). Given that all dance tunes of the Rolling Stones have spiritual underpinnings, their *credo* might be found the most clearly expressed in "Hot Stuff," a manifesto-like song structured on the Apocalypse of St. John with a Pentecostal guitar solo played by Harvey Mandel in which they announce their penultimate gospel: "This music is mighty mighty fine."

When asked why they continue to tour, Keith replied, "This whole thing runs on passion. ... Even though we don't talk about it much ourselves, it's almost a sort of quest or mission."

---

9 Andy Green, "Steve Jordan on Touring With the Stones: 'It Was Like Being Strapped to a Rocket Ship,'" *Rolling Stone*, December 6, 2021.

Artistic talent sometimes touches the inexplicable (Leonardo, Michelangelo, Bach, Mozart, and the Beatles). "Can't You Hear Me Knocking," one of the best tracks of jazz-rock fusion ever with a perfect architecture and a thrilling dramaturgy, is reportedly the fruit of coincidence. After recording the first 2:48 of the song, a rather classic rock piece, the band went on jamming, unaware that the microphones remained switched on. The result can be heard on *Sticky Fingers*. Stones recordings from the mid-1970s still sound as fresh and modern as if they were recorded today, with a timelessness that defies the laws of organic and aesthetic life. Maybe Bill Wyman had a point when he wrote in *Stone Alone*, "All this time some central force beyond music or money must have held us together."

SELECTED BIBLIOGRAPHY

Autobiographical writings

Jagger, Richards and Wood Watts. *According to the Rolling Stones.* Chronicle Books, San Francisco, 2009.

Loewenstein, Prince Rupert. *A Prince Among Stones, That Business with The Rolling Stones and Other Adventures.* Bloomsbury, London, 2013.

Oldham, Andrew. *Stoned.* Vintage, Random House, London, 2000.

Richards, Keith. *Life.* Weidenfeld & Nicolson, London, 2010.

Wood, Ronnie. *Ronnie. St.* MacMillan, London, 2007.

Wyman, Bill. *Stone Alone – The Story of a Rock 'n' Roll Band.* Viking, London, 1990.

Biographies

Andersen, Christoper. *Mick - The Wild Life and Mad Genius of Jagger.* Robson Press, London, 2012.

Bockris, Victor. *Keith.* Omnibus Press, New York, 2016.

Clayson, Alan. *Charlie Watts.* Sanctuary Books, London, 2004.

Jackson, Laura. *Brian Jones.* Piatkus, London, 2009.

Norman, Philip. *The Stones.* Harper, London, 2012.

Norman, Philip. *Mick Jagger.* Harper, London, 2012.

Sandford, Christopher. *The Rolling Stones- Fifty Years.* Simon & Schuster, London, 2013.

Other writings

Booth, Stanley. *The True Adventures of the Rolling Stones.* Canongate Books, Edinburgh, 2012.

Egan, Sean, ed. *Keith Richards on Keith Richards - Interview and Encounters.* Chicago Review Press, Chicago, 2013.

Egan, Sean, ed. *The Mammoth Book of the Rolling Stones.* Robinson, London, 2013.

Elliot, Martin. *Complete Recording Sessions 1962–2012.* Cherry Red Books, London, 2012.

Fornatale, Pete. *50 Licks - Myths and Stories from Half Century.* Bloomsbury, London, 2013.

Greenfield, Robert. *Exile on Main Street: A Season in Hell with the Rolling Stones.* Da Capo, Philadelphia, 2008.

Greenfield, Robert. *Stones Touring Party, A Journey Through America With the Rolling Stones.* Aurum Press, London, 1974.

Janovitz, Bill. *Rocks Off —50 Tracks that Tell the Story of the Rolling Stones.* St. Martin's Press, New York, 2013.

Serwer, Andy, Julia Boorstin, and Ann Harrington. "Inside the Rolling Stones Inc." *Fortune Magazine*, September 30, 2002.

Turner, Tina. *The Autobiography.* Century, London, 2018.

INDEX